Enjoying It

Candy Crush and Capitalism

Enjoying It

Candy Crush and Capitalism

Alfie Bown

Winchester, UK
Washington, USA

First published by Zero Books, 2015
Zero Books is an imprint of John Hunt Publishing Ltd., Laurel House, Station Approach,
Alresford, Hants, SO24 9JH, UK
office1@jhpbooks.net
www.johnhuntpublishing.com
www.zero-books.net

For distributor details and how to order please visit the 'Ordering' section on our website.

Text copyright: Alfie Bown 2014

ISBN: 978 1 78535 155 6
Library of Congress Control Number: 2015941038

A CIP catalogue record for this book is available from the British Library.

Design: Stuart Davies

Printed in the USA by Edwards Brothers Malloy

We operate a distinctive and ethical publishing philosophy in all
areas of our business, from our global network of authors to
production and worldwide distribution.

CONTENTS

Acknowledgements

Firstly I would like to thank my wife Kim, who I enjoy immensely and who has also given me many of the ideas that have gone into this book. Special thanks go to Doug Lain, for telling me an anecdote which confirmed to me that this was a book that needed writing. I would also like to thank the team at Everyday Analysis, who have tried to talk about enjoyment in as many ways as possible over the last few years. Further thanks go to James Smith for help with the manuscript and Joseph P. Kelly for the cover illustration. Finally, thanks to Jack Sullivan, Alexandre Pais and Tony Brown, for enjoying talking enjoyment with me many many times.

About the Author

Alfie Bown is editor of Everyday Analysis, a blog and book series with Zer0 Books available at everydayanalysis.com. He teaches English Literature at The University of Manchester, and writes on critical theory and comedy. He has written for several non-academic publications as well, including *The Guardian.*

0. Introduction: Enjoying This

God demands a *constant state of enjoyment,* such as would be
in keeping with the Order of Things.
– Judge Schreber[1]

I am really enjoying this: the process of writing an introduction
to a short book on enjoyment. I'm also looking forward to
finishing the introduction, so that I can return to an on-going
game of Football Manager that I am deeply invested in on my
new smartphone, which I am also definitely going to enjoy. In the
back of my mind is the possibility of having sex with my wife
later, which is a pastime I can realistically hope to derive intense
enjoyment from. Leaving behind any further over-sharing of the
biographical details of the author, which have been enjoyable to
share with the imaginary reader, this short book asks what, if
anything, connects these forms of enjoyment? How can we
discuss enjoyment and the differences between moments of
enjoyment? What would be the politics of doing so? And why is
this something we should do, or might *enjoy* doing?

The book argues that existing ways of discussing enjoyment
in our culture are not only insufficient but politically dangerous.
It argues that our language tends to organize enjoyment and
place what we might call value-judgements on it, legitimating
certain forms of enjoyment and dismissing others. This leaves us
in a bizarre second wave of what 19th-century Victorian
discourse called 'rational recreation,' a project that attempted to
impose and regulate leisure and enjoyment in order to contain
and limit revolutionary potential in its dissatisfied and potentially subversive subjects.[2]

In this book I look at this in light of 21st-century global
capitalism, arguing that we now see a divide between what we
might call 'productive' and 'unproductive' enjoyment.

Productive enjoyment can be thought of as enjoyment which serves our cultural and social structures, even though this kind of enjoyment can often seem like the most radical or anti-establishment form of enjoyment going. A subject enjoying his or her job (be that as an accountant or as a writer for an anti-establishment paper) could be an obvious but complicated example. Unproductive enjoyment, on the other hand, is that which we tend to think of as completely mindless and, oddly, as completely and merely *conformist* (but which, I argue, can nevertheless contain a radical moments which change the social order). A game of Angry Birds would be an obvious but complicated example. This apparently unproductive enjoyment, rather than mindless and ineffectual, can be a site at which ideology is powerfully imposed on its subjects.

In light of the fact that much radical potential in 'unproductive' enjoyment is ignored and much conformist compliance in 'productive' enjoyment goes unnoticed, I suggest that we need another way of discussing differences in experiences of enjoyment. In other words, we must dispel the idea that it is *necessarily* preferable or doing any more good for anyone when the author of this book enjoys writing his introduction than when he enjoys a six-hour stint on Football Manager. This understood, we can look for moments of enjoyment and ways of talking about them that really might be able to do something to influence our current unarable political landscape.

Enjoyment serves many ideological purposes, a major one being to enforce cultural divides between subjects from various classes and backgrounds, grouping people by what they enjoy and preventing communication across these enjoyment-divides. A new way of thinking about enjoyment would look for moments of enjoyment that are able to cross class divides and operate at cultural intersections to create new forms of resistance to the structures that try to organize our 'pleasure.' This book aims to discuss some types of enjoyment from Angry Birds to Aristotle without bringing a pre-conceived prejudice for one over the other. Whether the text in question is *Grazia* magazine, an interview with the singer of 'Gangnam Style' or postmodern European critical theory, they are used, it is hoped, in conversation with one another and without bias for one over the other. The perceived gap between enjoying philosophy and enjoying a tabloid newspaper is too great and is one of the things this book hopes to work against.

The first chapter discusses the ways in which seemingly radical moments of enjoyment are often coded within capitalist discourse and can be a form of conformation and adherence to the very structures that they see themselves as resisting. It discusses the enjoyment of reading and what this shows about contemporary (and class-specific) enjoyment of things that carry 'cultural capital.' As a kind of case study of this 'legitimate' enjoyment, the chapter discusses critical theory and how it is read, consumed and *enjoyed* as a commodity, despite its attempts to be an anti-capitalist and subversive form of resistance.

The second chapter discusses enjoyment that is often dismissed as uninteresting and nothing other than a sort of opiate of the masses, leaving us in what Walter Benjamin described as modernity's 'culture of distraction.'[3] This chapter shows how these seemingly banal moments of enjoyment can often be more transformative than meets the eye. The chapter discusses the enjoyments found in a 'culture of distraction' as recreation that is usually seen as completely opposite to something like the legitimately enjoyable reading of critical theory. The argument is not that Candy Crush and Angry Birds are truly radical but that they are truly transformative. Far from simply preventing us from doing 'useful' things, this kind of enjoyment has a serious ideological impact on us as modern subjects. It argues that rather than talking in terms of oppositions, this 'unproductive' enjoyment should be seen as a counterpart and an ally of the 'productive' enjoyment discussed in the first chapter. Together they show us two sides of how enjoyment is organized in our culture and both work to construct modern capitalist subjectivity.

The third chapter offers a new way of approaching enjoyment which does not fall prey to organizing enjoyment into what is legitimate/illegitimate, or what is radical/conformist. Using a particular strand of contemporary psychoanalysis (a field that anyone interested in how their culture works could do with being more engaged with) it suggests that enjoyment can be something that resists organization in a unique and special way. In short, it argues that certain moments of enjoyment reveal to us how we are constructed as subjects of modern capitalism, forcing us into a radical realization of our place in capitalist discourse. Here I use the psychoanalytic ideas of Jacques Lacan to show that rather than us choosing our enjoyment, our enjoyment chooses us and plays a key role in constructing us as subjects. Finally, the book looks at the future of enjoyment and of discussing enjoyment in an optimistic hope that we might break out of some of the capitalist ranking of enjoyment currently limiting our approach to the things we enjoy.

Enjoyment is the Key to Ideology

Enjoyment is a subject of academic study and of critical theory, and it has attracted people to critical theory and philosophy who might otherwise not have picked up these often alienating texts and enjoyed them. The embodiment of this *enjoyment* of reading 'critical theory' is of course Slavoj Žižek, a figure we enjoy watching and talking about while he enjoys discussing enjoyment and subjecting it to his special brand of Žižekian-Slovenian-Lacanian philosophical analysis. In his wonderful introduction to Žižek, Ian Parker explains that 'many readers found themselves bewitched and fascinated by something inside [Žižek's] first book,' and that 'the attraction to Žižek was already operating fairly efficiently as a political factor in the *enjoyment* of a growing readership of leftist cultural theorists' [emphasis added].[4] All this, at the same time that Žižek himself was discussing all sorts of other forms of enjoyment in our society: cinema, TV, games, laughter and sex. The question we need to be asking is whether there two forms of enjoyment here: one, something enjoyed by 'the masses,' Hollywood films for example, perhaps enjoyed blindly and uncritically (at least most of the time); and another, something enjoyed by a leftist or at least literary culture, found in the taking apart and analysis of enjoyment. Would this map onto the enjoyment felt by the author when writing this book versus the enjoyment he might feel when he plays Football Manager later? Is there anything sexual about either enjoyment to connect them to yet another type of enjoyment or to show that they might share a root cause (a question traditional psychoanalysis might ask)? These are questions I come back to in my 'case studies' of critical theory and Football Manager below.

Žižek's main point about enjoyment has been made very clearly and has been subsumed within many subsequent approaches to enjoyment inside and outside the academy. Žižek's work aimed to show how the Freudian idea of the superego as something that says 'no,' prohibiting you from accessing enjoyment (from the primary suckling on the mother's teat right through to advanced cultural enjoyments you can access in adult life), was something of an over-simplification and misleadingly risked implying that our desires and enjoyments are natural impulses that are then regulated and prohibited by the social injunctions to 'stop.'[5] The idea, as is so often the case the with Žižek's work, comes directly from Jacques Lacan, who wrote that 'nothing forces anyone to enjoy except the superego. The superego is the imperative of *jouissance* (pleasure) — Enjoy!'[6] Freud's regulatory agency was not simply there to stop you enjoying, but rather demanded that you partake in enjoyment, at least of certain kinds. Yet, it was Žižek's insistence on this point that showed how important it was to reverse the way we see the relationship between enjoyment and the superego. This was because the existing view risked *naturalizing* our desires and our relationships to the things we want or enjoy; it allowed us to think of desire as natural and society as the prohibiting force preventing us from having what we truly desire. Instead, Žižek showed that at least in our modern Western society almost the opposite is true, and that we should see the main command of the superego as the command to 'enjoy.'

But this has itself been a misunderstood position. It needs to be stressed that the point is not so much that society tells us *what* to enjoy (though it does), but that it tells us *to enjoy* per se. This seems important given how often we are given an impression that it doesn't matter what we enjoy, just that we do. Social media seems to make this ring truer than ever, with both Facebook and Instagram appearing not so much like a competition to be more 'successful' than our peers, as a recent edition of *Grazia* magazine (a complex form of enjoyment itself) reported, but a competition to be *enjoying* more, a battle to show that we are enjoying more things and enjoying them more often than anyone else on our newsfeed.[7] The quotation with which this chapter began is from Freud's discussion of the Schreber case and embodies this way in which constant enjoyment is the command from God and supports the 'order of things.' As long as we can say that we are 'enjoying ourselves,' our choices must be accepted by others, and we appear to have the approval of the state (or God) for our actions. This is all relatively self-evident and it is hard to imagine an argument that our condition in the West today is not one best characterized by this command to enjoy. The question we need to be asking is why it is that modern capitalism tells its subjects to 'enjoy' in the way it does? One potential answer might be that the more we conform to the command to enjoy, the more we are encouraged to increase expenditure on enjoyable things, in turn promoting the market.

In a very interesting book which shares something with this one, Lacanian Todd McGowan argues that today's society, 'rather than demanding that its members give up their individual enjoyment for the sake of the whole' (as society has historically worked), functions instead through 'the demand that we maximize our enjoyment.' For McGowan, today 'private enjoyment becomes of paramount importance' while 'the importance of the social order as a whole seems to recede.'[8] Following Žižek, McGowan argues that we now see a new 'mode of subjectivity that corresponds to global capitalism,' which we can call 'pathological narcissism,' a subject for whom 'duty is transformed into a duty to enjoy' and who spends freely into the market of capital as a result of this compulsion. McGowan focuses on parallels between the structure of capitalism and the structure of enjoyment, and there are many. He writes, for instance, that 'by allowing subjects easy and fast credit, today's corporations create avenues through which subjects can pursue their enjoyment. In fact, the very idea of the emergence of a society of enjoyment is unthinkable without a credit-based economy.'[9] The focus then, is on how the capitalist system has made enjoyment work in its favor, an argument which is shared here. Having said that, there are also two significant differences of approach. First, this book is interested in various forms of enjoyment and how they serve particular aspects of the system in place at this particular moment. Second, whilst these arguments suggest that the subject is encouraged to be unregulated, at least in the following of its enjoyments which involve expenditure in the service of capitalism, it is argued here that there is also a way in which enjoyment is completely regulated even at the very moment when we seem to be more encouraged to enjoy all and everything than ever, a way in which we are nowhere near as 'free to enjoy' as we might think.

Speaking of laughter, the less well-known but equally interesting Slovenian-Lacanian philosopher Mladen Dolar writes:

Laughter is the condition of ideology. It provides us with the distance, the very space in which ideology can take its full swing. It is only with laughter that we become ideological subjects [...] It is only when we laugh and breathe freely that ideology truly has a hold on us.[10]

Likewise, when we are enjoying, we feel we are freely being ourselves. Because we feel we haven't chosen what we enjoy, that instead it has chosen us, we feel it is something about us that causes us to enjoy it. We become invested in our enjoyment, because it seems to be a symptom of ourselves, it seems tied to our deepest nature. French theorist Pierre Bourdieu has made this point in relation to the idea of 'taste' in the most compelling way, and his work sheds light on our discussion here. For Bourdieu, taste is completely culturally acquired, which is nothing new. He writes: 'whereas the ideology of charisma regards taste in legitimate culture as a gift of nature, scientific observation shows that cultural needs are the product of upbringing and education.' His important contribution is to point out that the role of taste in our culture depends on *forgetting* the 'learned' nature of taste, leaving us feeling that we have a natural gift for appreciating the things we find palatable. For Bourdieu, we are left with 'an enchanted experience of culture which implies forgetting the acquisition.'[11] In other words, our enjoyment of culture works by making us forget that we have acquired it. In this way, enjoyment is the key to ideology, making socialized things *feel* natural.

The first question of this book is why it should be '*enjoy*' that is the central cultural injunction of modern capitalism. Why so much enjoyment? Why is it less important *what* we enjoy but *that* we enjoy? Perhaps here is the first indication that there are differences too between the present and the 19th-century project of rational recreation, where it was always the type of enjoyment that was important. Here is my provisional conclusion then:

enjoyment operates as has been discussed here by applying ideas from Žižek, Dolar and Bourdieu to the context of modern enjoyment. Enjoyment constructs us culturally but also makes us feel an enchanted sense of freedom and 'a gift of nature,' instilling the idea of a natural and individualist self which is free to enjoy and whose enjoyment is a symptom of its self. This makes it the ideal instruction to be issued from our ideology and it also explains why it is more important *that* we enjoy than *what* we enjoy. In short, the more we experience enjoyment in this way, the more we become individualist capitalist subjects. To be in the 'constant state of enjoyment' described by Schreber is to be the perfect capitalist subject, not only always enjoying but always enjoying as if it is in our nature to do so. The second task of the book is to look for elements of enjoyment that can do something against this force of constructing and sustaining modern subjectivity.

1. Productive Enjoyment: Capitalism and Critical Theory

> The work of art undertakes to produce entertainment in a responsible manner.
> – Walter Benjamin[12]

This chapter discusses how a great deal of enjoyment which appears to be radical and questioning of normative or dominant ideology can in fact serve those ideologies it aims to oppose. The chapter does this though a discussion of how critical theory is read and enjoyed. I hope the discussion can also shed light on other forms of enjoyment that are considered legitimate and even radical, so 'critical theory' operates as a kind of case study here. Though of course completely different forms, art-house film or acclaimed 'literary fiction' could have provided comparable examples. The chapter argues that despite the potential radicalism of the theory itself, it can be and often is enjoyed in a way that does nothing more than conform to the social injunction to enjoy that was discussed above as a way of establishing a subjectivity that suits modern capitalism.

Some of the categories that we might think of as legitimate enjoyment are independent film, art, theory and literature. These are all examples of enjoyment that we can be 'proud' to define ourselves by or enjoyment that carries 'cultural capital,' and all of them are value judgements. This is nothing new, and much academic study has been dedicated to showing this. They are all 'culture' in the way it was discussed by figures from Matthew Arnold in the 19th-century to one of the fathers of literary criticism, F. R. Leavis, in the 1930s and 40s. Arnold famously defined culture as 'the best that has be thought or said,' and for Leavis there is a:

minority capable not only of appreciating Dante, Shakespeare, Baudelaire, Hardy (to take major instances) but of recognizing their latest successors constitute the consciousness of the race (or of a branch of it) at a given time. Upon this minority depends our power of profiting by the finest human experience of the past; they keep alive the subtlest and most perishable parts of tradition. Upon them depend the implicit standards that order the finer living of an age, the sense [...] that the centre is here rather than there. In their keeping is the language, the changing idiom upon which fine living depends, and without which distinction of spirit is thwarted and incoherent. By 'culture' I mean the use of such language.[13]

Leavis is much misunderstood and misused by those in literary studies who celebrate their own supposed progress from the ideas expressed here; Leavis is taken as the embodiment of the problematic endorser of the 'literary canon' that right-on literary critics like to imagine they have now moved beyond. As literary and critical theorists such as Terry Eagleton have long since pointed out, 'anything can be literature, and anything which is regarded as unalterably and unquestionably literature – Shakespeare, for example – can cease to be literature,' meaning that 'there is no such thing as a literary work or tradition which is valuable *in itself*, regardless of what anyone might have said or come to say about it.'[14] Most universities teach this point to first-year undergraduate students as an introduction to theory, and there is nothing new in repeating it here in the context not only of literature but of a wider range of forms of enjoyment that seem to be culturally 'legitimate' in the same way that 'literature' is simply writing that passes some test of legitimacy. It is obvious that in some ways enjoyment has been canonized and organized in a similar way. The point that needs making is that unlike with literature and art, when it comes to what we enjoy, any value judgement we make is (at least usually) unconscious. As discussed in the introduction, Pierre Bourdieu's idea of 'taste' holds a key here, showing that whilst our taste is completely learned and culturally determined, we forget this and imagine that our taste is instinctive. What we see with the regulation of enjoyment is that we are not as free as we think from Leavis's 'backwardness.' In other words, when we choose what to enjoy, our unconscious mind is just as organized and judgemental as Leavis's conscious mind, but we are not in control of this judgement.

The chapter will now look at the enjoyment of reading in light of this, discussing critical theory as something one has to develop a taste for, and asking whether the enjoyment of it does not involve something like Bourdieu's idea of an enchanted experience in which we forget the cultural acquisition of our taste and enjoy the material as though we have a 'gift of nature' allowing us to enjoy it: an almost natural connection to what we enjoy. By calling this chapter 'productive enjoyment' I suggest that this enjoyment, though it aims to be non-conformist, can end up *producing* subjectivities that suit a capitalist and individualist agenda.

There is a general sense that the enjoyment of reading critical theory is not only legitimate but also radical and opposed to the normative structures in place in our capitalist society, as if the fact that someone enjoys critical theory shows that they are at some deep level at odds with capitalism. Enjoyment plays a key role in the construction of this appearance, since it is the fact that the material is enjoyed that adds the appearance of depth to the subjectivity doing the enjoying. Whilst reading and working on critical theory (without it mattering whether this is found enjoyable) is or can be an act of political resistance, it is when enjoyment comes in that the identity of the anarchist is established: if someone finds critical theory hard work and near-impossible to break into, or they 'don't get it,' they are perceived of (from within critical theory circles) as somehow conformist, whereas if one 'enjoys' critical theory they are imagined to possess that 'gift of nature' that makes them a radical subject at odds with 'the system.' Our ideas surrounding the enjoyment of critical theory and political resistance lead to the celebrated *identity of the radical*, which is another way of being a subject that suits capitalism (constantly enjoying and with a natural taste for what is enjoyed) and not the kind of subjectivity that much critical theory would like to promote at all. In his famous essay 'What is an Author?' Michel Foucault, a major advocate of Deleuze (discussed below), describes how capitalism, by imposing the identity and ownership rights that come with the label of 'author,' has limited the transgressive potential of the writer.[15] With enjoyment, it is as if the reader acquires ownership rights too, seeing the text as their own and affirming their identity through it, reducing the transgressive potential of the reader too. Despite the reams of 'reader response theory,' no one seems to have quite made this point that the reader is similarly commodified.

Of course, critical theory can and does offer new ways of thinking about political and cultural structures that resist existing shibboleths in the language we have to discuss our political situation, and this is not in any kind of dispute here. The two examples of critical theory discussed here contribute to the exploration of how enjoyment in our society is rationalized and regulated, seeking alternatives to these structures. Without any criticism of the theorists discussed, the point is that the enjoyment of this critical theory indicates that the material is often consumed and enjoyed as a product in precisely the way the theories in question would oppose, and in precisely the way the structures that they attempt to resist would command. The two examples of theory discussed below should not be read as a commentary on those theorists themselves, nor as an attempt to contribute to academic work on these theorists, but as small 'case studies' of how their work is enjoyed in relation to a few of the key ideas that each theorist has developed. This analysis is partly about the study of enjoyment, but it is also about the enjoyment of studying. In these case studies, the theorists will be used against the grain of their own enjoyment to show that the systems of enjoyment that they help to make visible to us are so deeply entrenched that the enjoyment of their own texts is often dictated by these systems.

Case Study 1: Deleuze and Guattari

Some of the most enjoyable critical theorists to read are almost certainly Gilles Deleuze and Felix Guattari. Their texts, the most famous and popular of which are the two volumes of *Capitalism and Schizophrenia*, are written in an enticing and creative style which feels both modernist and postmodernist, though they are careful to distance their arguments from the latter on certain points. Their theory could not be more directly against the individualist identities that suit capitalism, arguing (as the title of their collection suggests) that whilst the modern subject is instructed to think of itself as singular and individual, it is in fact completely schizophrenic, a multiple and split subject. This is an idea that helps to explore the function of enjoyment in the 21st century (see Case Study 2 of this section).

There is a definite connection between these enjoyable books and the theories put forward within them. For Deleuze and Guattari, subjects should be seen as 'desiring machines' which derive pleasure from plugging themselves into all sorts of other desiring machines, which can be anything from other humans to the natural world to cultural and media entertainment. Which machines we plug into is organized by our social discourse. For Deleuze and Guattari, the key way in which capitalism organizes its subjects is through an organization of desire. They argue that whilst desire exists outside of capitalism, it is not a desire *for* something until cultural factors and discourses map and channel desire into articulable and organized directions, turning unregulated desire into desire that serves the purposes of capital by directing it towards an object, making us desire *things*.

Much of Deleuze and Guattari's work, as indicated by their title *Anti-Oedipus*, makes a criticism of psychoanalysis on the grounds that psychoanalysis is guilty of normalizing a certain fixed structure of the subject and implying that this is the only way that a subject could be formed. In speaking of the subject as being structured in a particular way, psychoanalysis can be guilty of foreclosing on the possibility of the subject being formed in other alternative ways. A central idea for their discussion and for this argument is the idea of 'lack.' It is lack that makes us, as capitalist subjects, desire a multitude of *things* which we imagine on some level will fulfil us or prevent us feeling that we are lacking something. Even if we know the iPhone 5 will not really complete us, we still desire it as if it will.

Deleuze and Guattari's critique of psychoanalysis[16] hinges on the fact that whilst psychoanalysis sees this lack as originary and all desire as a subsequent relation to this original lack (so that we desire the things we are lacking), Deleuze and Guattari see a possibility of desire that precedes any organization of the subject, arguing in opposition to Lacan that 'lack is a counter-effect of desire.'[17] For them, desire comes first and is channeled and regulated so that it appears to be the result of lack. This is a very important point because for psychoanalysis the construction of the modern subject as a lacking being is the key part of its formation and all later experiences of enjoyment are in relation to this originary or formational lack. I will return to this in chapter 3 where psychoanalysis and enjoyment are discussed in detail.

For now what is important is that Deleuze and Guattari propose an experience of desire that is not to do with the subject and anything like its 'fulfilment,' which would be an idea of enjoyment based on the subject as lacking and of the things we enjoy as promising or simulating fulfilment (previous and many subsequent discussions of enjoyment have relied on this assumption). Instead, this experience of desire would break out of the structure of subjectivity given to us by capitalism. It sheds light on some of what we imagine to be 'productive' enjoyment, since this would be an enjoyment that is not only unproductive but completely against systems of production. In *Anti-Oedipus* Deleuze and Guattari write:

> Desire does not lack anything; it does not lack its object. It is, rather, the *subject* that is missing in desire, or desire that lacks a fixed subject; there is no fixed subject unless there is repression.[18]

In short, for Deleuze and Guattari, once desire has an 'object,' once desire is for *things*, the subject is already formed and structured as a subject. Outside this structure would be a desire in which 'the subject is missing.' Though it is something of a jump to connect desire to enjoyment, it might still be possible to think of what a Deleuzian enjoyment would look like, an enjoyment in which 'the subject is missing.'

Deleuze and Guattari discuss the idea of a '*desire-delirium*,' an unregulated experience of desire that is not a desire *for* something or directed towards an object, which would always be within a culturally mapped and organized subjectivity, but a moment where existing subjectivity is relinquished and 'missing.' In this light it might be possible to see the subject as an 'enjoying machine,' plugging into various other machines and experiencing what Deleuze and Guattari might call an 'enjoyment-delirium,' enjoyment that changes the subject or threatens its stability. There would be a danger, though, in thinking that this enjoyment could be outside capital or organization (since it is often when we think we are outside of ideology that it operates most powerfully on us) and even more of a danger if a divide is made between conformist and resistant enjoyments (since it would involve a value-judgement privileging one over the other). These risks aside, I later argue that the enjoyment we experience when watching 'Gangnam Style' might be thought of in this way as an *enjoyment without a subject*, but here the point is that the enjoyment of Deleuze's texts is often as far from this dream of an enjoyment without a subject as possible; the enjoyment of Deleuze often re-affirms the kind of subjectivity that Deleuze himself opposes.

Perhaps this can be thought of in terms of the enjoyment of the Deleuzian text itself. Deleuzian theory posits the idea of a limiting structure in which our desires are channeled and it proposes that we break out of these confines or at least open up the theoretical possibility of doing do. This is an over-simplified way of explaining Deleuze and Guattari's famous terms 'deterritorialization' and 'reterritorialization,' a breaking down of territorialized boundaries and confines acting on the subject and the openness to the formation of new structures in their place.[19] For the reader, the experience of the text may mirror this (certainly if the text is working as Deleuze and Guattari might hope), and a feeling of enjoyment reading the text might have to do with a shift in subjectivity that the text aims not only to affirm but to achieve. It seems, on the one hand, that the way the theory is enjoyed is in perfect alignment with what the theory is expounding, and this point may go some way to explaining the popularity of Deleuze and Guattari both inside and outside of the academy. Enjoying Deleuze is seen by many as a breaking out of normative structures.

On the other hand, the points made above through Žižek ask that we look at this in yet another way. If Žižek shows that the main command of the superego is the command to 'enjoy,' then do we not see a conformation to this in our experiences of enjoying critical theory, a desire to enjoy the process of reading and working on theory, and a feeling that there might also be something radical in this enjoyment of working and reading? It is important to us that we should 'enjoy it,' but is this enjoyment really something we can positively invest in as a radical experience of shifting subjectivity? It may in some cases be just that, but it may also be (and perhaps at the same time) an enchanting experience of an individualist 'gift of nature' in which we forget that we have learned to enjoy the material and feel that it chimes with our identities and affirms our sense of a subject with radical potential experiencing a self-affirming affinity with the text.[20] Most of the time when we enjoy Deleuze and Guattari we cannot say that 'the subject is missing' at all but that it is affirmed as a radical subject with legitimate taste.

Deleuze and Guattari's critique of psychoanalysis is the most compelling in a long history of criticisms and is worthy of a sustained study of its own. They argue that psychoanalysis is too dependent on the idea that we are lacking subjects, given that 'lack is created, planned, and organized in and through social production.'[21] The way that we think in terms of lack is part of the identity given to us by the conditions of our culture, a key way in which our desires are controlled and channeled. This may be a position that psychoanalysis needs to take up, since it is a valid point that psychoanalysis only discusses a certain form of subjectivity which is predicated on a feeling of lack which the subject desires to fill or avoid. However, perhaps the point to be made here is that if desire can be prior to lack (as it is for Deleuze), then enjoyment cannot be. In other words, between desire and enjoyment, in the moment desire becomes enjoyment through its social organization, the subject runs through a process that constructs them as lacking. I am with Deleuze here, then, in seeing the particular kind of enjoyment posited by psychoanalysis as only something experienced by the (post)modern Western subjectivity. However, the way Deleuze himself is consumed and enjoyed is no different; it certainly does not escape the organization of the modern Western and capitalist subject. We could put it in the following way: the way that we enjoy Deleuze is precisely as a lacking subject seeking to affirm its identity, which is exactly the kind of enjoyment that Deleuze and Guattari would oppose.

The Deleuze Facebook group is one of the most entertaining sites on the internet, and it is hard to resist quoting at length the discussions, arguments and numerous instances of borderline bullying that go on within this group that has a relatively modest six thousand or so followers. It is important that the group is populated by both those with a popular interest in Deleuze and by academics and writers who work on Deleuze, and judging from the group, the distinction between those two is almost negligible. Many quotes and status updates by Deleuze fans testify to the 'gift of nature' I have discussed here, with comments including: 'I don't want to interpret Deleuze, I want to be like him. I want to use him to be me.' The individual dimension of our enjoyment of Deleuze is clear, even when the theory itself would oppose such an idea. The responses to these comments, though, are even more remarkable, with comments such as 'Deleuze would never have said that,' followed by a really quite alarming number of insults and expletives fairly common on the site. Perhaps this shows again the regulation of the type of enjoyment found here, that an individual can be hounded for enjoying the material 'illegitimately.' The other major thing that we cannot avoid noticing on Deleuze-themed social-media sites is the surprising amount of photographs uploaded showing people reading Deleuze, usually whilst lying in bed or on the beach. Here we have a clear indication of the *fetishization of literature* in our culture. For Lacan, following Freud, the fetish is that which covers up the lack felt by the subject.[22] This can be thought of in sexual terms but it also applies to discussions of commodity fetishism in Marxism. The book is enjoyed as a commodity (like any other) that will work towards our fulfilment, which promises to complete us, which helps the subject 'to be me.' What we see is that the enjoyment of Deleuze is well within a structure of the modern subject that is organized around a sense of lack and the possibility of fulfilment. In short, we see that there is very often nothing Deleuzian about our way of enjoying Deleuze.

Case Study 2: Jean-Francois Lyotard

Another theorist to talk extensively about enjoyment, and to be immensely enjoyed, is Jean-Francois Lyotard, a theorist who is much less read and taught than he should be. He seems to have suffered from a connection to postmodernism and a sense that he invests too heavily in the postmodern world he writes about, which has meant his work has gone out of fashion. The fashion-like quality of critical theory studies would itself be worthy of attention, but for now it's enough to say that Lyotard, like Lacan, is not '*in*, this season.' This may be because these theorists have been 'explained away' by the university discourse (see chapter 3 for more). Lyotard's analysis of the postmodern subject, however, is complex and insightful. Like Deleuze, Lyotard discusses the idea of *lack* as central to the formation of the modern subject of capitalism. Yet there is a key difference between Deleuze and Lyotard when it comes to discussions of enjoyment. Whilst Deleuzian theory raises the question of an 'enjoyment' that is outside the law, Lyotard, like other critical theorists, suggests that there is enjoyment found in being subjected to the law and the subject positions ordained within it.

Some previous discussions of Lyotard have touched on some of the discussions here. Fredric Jameson's famous argument – that postmodernism, whilst it conceives of itself as a resistance or response to the conditions of capitalist modernity, might in fact be seen as the 'cultural logic of late capitalism,' a symptom of the culture it sees itself as resisting – has been related (by Jameson himself) to Lyotard's work.[23] Jameson's argument seems to have stopped further discussions of Lyotard and operated to close his text. Nevertheless, it is possible to get somewhere by applying Jameson's critique to the idea of enjoyment; it would suggest that the celebration of split and multiple identities in postmodern theory replicates postmodern capitalism's need for its subjects to enjoy the multiple and contradictory things that it sells. If we are constructed as split-subjects, we can spend our money on contradictory and diverse enjoyments without needing to construct any narratives linking them together. The situation Jameson describes might also prevent us from drawing links between seemingly diverse forms of enjoyment and seeing how they often supplement each other and how there are unconscious narratives connecting different types of enjoyment (see the argument of chapter 2, that our enjoyment of work and our enjoyment of Candy Crush have an inherent link).

The point that we are told to enjoy multiple and often contradictory things helps highlight the question that needs asking: why is there is such a cultural injunction to enjoy, even if what we are enjoying does not seem to serve the agenda of the market, as when we enjoy the cultural critique of Lyotard or Deleuze? Our enjoyment of these things still seems to do something to satisfy the demands of the superego. Enjoying Lyotard and Deleuze, as critiques of capitalism, works on one level against the conditions of our system and creates new languages for resistance, but it can also completely conform to the prescribed enjoyments of our moment and fall into re-enforcing the order it seeks to dislodge.

In *Libidinal Economy,* a title that addresses the capitalist organization of desire, suggesting that even our libidinal desires and drives are regulated, economized and made use of by ideology, Lyotard writes:

> The reintroduction of the Zero, that is to say, of the negative, in the economy of desire, is quite simply that of accountancy in libidinal matters; it is political economy, that is, capital,

carried even into the sphere of the passions [...] This is identified as the *force of lack*, capitalist religiosity, which is that of money engendering itself, *causa sui*.[24]

For Lyotard, the introduction of the idea of lack into our consciousness is the most capitalist thing going. The economy of politics and capital works first and foremost by introducing lack to the subject, creating the subject as a lacking being whose desires can then be organized around the promise of compensation for this lack. The subject of psychoanalysis would be a subject within such capitalist organization. Enjoyment for Lyotard, as for psychoanalysis, is experienced inside this structure and in relation to it. In Lyotard's terms:

The passage through the zero is itself a particular libidinal course, [and] the position of the Signifier or of the Other is [...] itself an enjoyable [*jouissive*] position. The rigour of the law gives more than one person a hard-on.[25]

Again, enjoyment is channeled and organized by the idea of lack, described here as 'the passage through the zero,' the subject's development through the introduction of the absent or missing that makes it lacking. The 'libidinal course' is the channeling and mapping of desire by ideology and it produces subject-positions. These subject-positions are imposed by the rigor of the law and Lyotard describes them as 'terroristic.' Yet, each position is found enjoyable or *jouissive* (see chapter 3 on *jouissance*). The law 'gives more than one person a hard-on,' meaning that both the subject imposing the law and the subject on whom the law is imposed find enjoyment in their master/slave positions.

This leads to another important point that Lyotard makes about enjoyment: that discussions of capitalism themselves become enjoyable. In a fascinating discussion of Marx, Lyotard discusses how in the process of writing *Capital*, Marx's text increasingly grew with 'a chapter becoming a book, a section a chapter, a paragraph a section.' Lyotard reads this as an increasing fascination with capitalism and with discussing it. He writes:

> What happens when the person assigned to the prosecution is as fascinated by the accused as he is scandalised by him? It comes about that the prosecutor sets himself to finding a hundred thousand good reasons to prolong the study of the file, that the enquiry becomes meticulous, always more meticulous, that the lawyer submerged in the British Museum in the microscopic analysis of the aberrations of capital is no longer able to detach himself from it.[26]

This is not a critique of Marx, and Lyotard dislikes 'critique' as a discourse and writes that 'there is no need to criticise Marx.'[27] Capitalism here is the 'accused' and Marx, or any criticism of capitalism, is the 'prosecution.' There is an enjoyment in the critique of capitalism and in the position of being subjected to its laws and this may be comparable with the 'enjoyable' position of the Other in the previous quotation. Yet, there is more to it than this and a close reading of the two passages in relation to each other is necessary. The legal language is important because it reverses the 'rigour of the law' as the force of capitalism operating on its subjects, turning the anti-capitalist subject into the 'prosecutor' who accuses capitalism and asks it to account for itself as a defendant. The positions of the previous quotation are therefore reversed with the critiquing subject switching from slave to master. Both of these positions are enjoyable. There is no sense of an eradication of the capitalism order here and instead criticism becomes nothing more than 'the microscopic analysis of the aberrations of capital' that becomes part of it and unable 'to detach' itself from it.

Lyotard's argument offers an insight into how political and

critical writing is consumed and enjoyed, and can be brought to bear on the increasingly common critiques of capitalism that fill our newspapers and bookshelves in the 21st century. Whilst there is a need for critique and whilst it has much subversive potential, there is also a danger of it falling into this trap of being subsumed within the system it operates against. At the very least, our *enjoyment* of such texts needs to be analyzed and assessed as much as, if not more than, the content of the text itself. This book itself is an example, and if it has been even a little bit enjoyable to read (certainly it has been enjoyable to write) then it may be because it has taken up the position of 'prosecutor' and put capitalism in the dock, enjoying this structure of enjoyment that is given to it by the laws of the very system it resists. In our own enjoyment of the material we can learn as much about ourselves and about the construction and the formation of the capitalist subject as in the arguments put forward by the text.

The epigraph to this chapter is a quotation from Walter Benjamin raising the idea that the 'work of art' involves a regulated kind of enjoyment that we can think of as 'enjoying responsibly,' or in other words, rationally. I have taken 'responsibly' and 'rationally' here to mean *in accordance with existing and approved thought*, just as the Victorian insistence that recreation ought to be 'rational' was an attempt to ensure no new forms of thought came into being and the old ones were affirmed. In these terms, this chapter has argued that critical theory can embody this function of the work of art. Whilst critical theory can be radically transformative, it is often enjoyed far more 'responsibly' than we think. Our consumption of Deleuze and Lyotard involves fetishizing and identifying with the material, the very things these text would warn against. This is by no means a criticism of these kinds of enjoyment, and certainly there is no unproblematic enjoyment of the material to aim for. The point is that in the interstices between the text and the enjoyment experienced when reading it, the construction of the subject can become visible to us. The chapter began by discussing how the enjoyment of 'subversive' material appears to construct the subject as a subversive opponent to capitalism. Instead, the text ought always to be great against the grain of its enjoyment, our own enjoyment often showing not our resistance to the structures of our capitalist society but our complicity within it. The enjoyment therefore is *productive* of capitalist subjectivity.

2. Unproductive Enjoyment: 'A Culture of Distraction'

> There have been days (more often than I'd like to admit) when I have given more to my Football Manager life than to my real life. But that's how you win the Champions League with Lille.
> – Jack Phillips[28]

What follows is an analysis of modernity as the world of 'distraction.' I argue that this 'distracting' enjoyment is a counterpart to the above idea of 'worthwhile' or 'fulfilling' enjoyment, and not its opposite, as is often supposed. So much is our society thought of as a culture of distraction that Attention Deficit Disorder (ADD) has come to be thought of as a *maladie du siècle* and has been discussed across a huge number of discourses from medicine to the arts as a phenomenon that characterizes our culture.[29] We scarcely have a moment free of distraction, and the number of these distractions that demand our enjoyment is obviously significant. Just as critical theory was used in the above discussion to stand in for a kind of enjoyment that is often thought of as useful, legitimate and even radical, here mobile-phone games will be used as an example of an enjoyment that is seen as nothing more than a distraction and an unproductive use of time. I argue here that it is of political importance to realize that this enjoyment is anything but unproductive and in fact should be seen as particularly productive form of modern subjectivity. This is not meant in any positive way. Rather, we must see that there is an organized and organizing agenda behind the effects that these forms of apparently innocent enjoyment produce.

These enjoyable distractions, I argue, cannot be discussed without reference to the workplace. The regular enjoyment of 'distracting' and 'unproductive' entertainment is a vital part of determining our relationship to 'work.' It may also relate to the medicalization of dissent and alienation as 'work stress,' and the turn to these forms of distracting enjoyment as an alternative to or distraction from work dissatisfaction. These forms of enjoyment are part of categorizing work as unenjoyable and also ensuring that this unenjoyable work continues unquestioned. As soon as no compulsion to work exists, it is 'shunned like the plague' in favor of Buzzfeed, Candy Crush and Football Manager. I argue here that like the medicalization of work dissent, 'distracting' enjoyment works to hide alienation and prevent organized rejection of working conditions.

The two case studies that follow look at two very different kinds of a culture of distraction. Superficially, these two types of enjoyment are very much related, since both Candy Crush and Football Manager Handheld are mobile-phone games that aim to distract us and to pass our time, snatch any moments of potential boredom or indeed reflection, leaving us in a constant state of entertainment. They ensure that there is no reason not to be enjoying, even as we wait for our train or bus, for our computer to power up or for our friends to meet us. With Candy Crush and Football Manager, Schreber's fears appear to be truly realized. However, these two mobile-phone games in fact show us two different sides of our 'culture of distraction' and how it functions.

To distinguish the key difference between the two we can make use of the Lacanian-Žižekian idea of the big Other. The idea of the superego was discussed above and the big Other is a related but crucially different concept. Whilst the superego issues the command to enjoy, the big Other ensures that this enjoyment is seen and approved. The big Other is a god-like figure who appears to watch over us and has the power to ensure our conformation to the order of things. The big Other is of course completely imaginary and can only appear to exist if we act as if it is there, which we almost invariably do. In other words, we can only speak of 'the system' because we act as if it is there and obey it, so that to all intents and purposes, it really is there. The idea is nicely summarized by Lacanian Daniel Bristow, who writes:

> We may be more familiar with the reference to the 'system' – certainly in terms of *surveillance culture* – as *Big Brother*, or, indeed, even by the reduction of it to the figure of the *Nanny*, as in the mythologized notion of the 'Nanny State'. However [...] the big Other is, in effect, that which we 'keep up appearances' for, and it is, therefore, bigger than all of us. It is the symbolic matrix that relies on us for its maintenance: our courtesy in everyday exchanges, our politeness, our following rules and abiding by the law, our leading by example are all for – in Lacan's view – this radical other, the 'big Other.'[30]

The big Other appears to watch what we do, guaranteeing our conformation but also, and more importantly for the argument here, affirming our actions and identities, offering assurances that what we do is approved and legitimized. We seek affirmation more often from this big Other than we do from any concrete 'other' (an individual for example) who we know in our social lives. Social media would once more be a case in point, where it often matters less which 'likes' and 're-tweets' we get or from whom we get them, and more that we do get them from somewhere. In some cases, what we send out to be seen by the other on social media may not be noticed, or even seen, by any individual (on Twitter especially) but we nonetheless feel it has been seen by the imaginary big Other and affirmed. We feel as though something has been publicly displayed and we imagine public approval.

In the two case studies below, one depends entirely on the imaginary approval of the big Other, where the other hopes to hide from the big Other, but each ultimately amounts to the same thing, as I will now show.

Case Study 1: The Candy Crush Saga

Discussing the mobile-phone game Angry Birds in an article for Everyday Analysis, I tried to investigate the idea that when we play mobile-phone games (on trains, buses, secretly at work, in waiting rooms), viewed by almost everyone as a tempting distraction from 'real stuff,' we partly enjoy doing so on the level that the associated guilt actually re-enforces our sense of being very important people with 'much more important things to do.'[31] The distraction supplements that mundane but supposed-to-be serious reality from which we secretly want to be distracted, allowing us to feel that what we 'should' be doing (usually working) is truly 'worthwhile.'

In this light it is definitely amusing that David Cameron, a man who must have had anxieties about the worthiness of his work, has completed Angry Birds, a fact reported on by almost every major UK news outlet.[32] It is this type of thing that earned him the caricature of Britain's first 'chillaxing prime minister.'[33] Perhaps this poses a different kind of threat to our political structure than the one brilliantly suggested by a 2013 article in *The Mirror* entitled 'David Cameron's Angry Birds addiction may be a threat to the nation's security,' in which it was feared that his personal data would be hacked through the game's server.[34] Certainly the mass reporting of our Prime Minister's enjoyment shows that we are in a deeply problematic political climate that is concerned more with the identity of the person we are voting for than with their policies. In 2015, an ITN series on the major party leaders attempted to give an insight into 'who they really are' by looking at their enjoyments, such as Nick Clegg's enjoyment of Ellie Goulding or Nigel Farage's love of skinny-dipping. What we enjoy is seen as a reflection of our deepest identities, an idea that this book strongly objects to. We ought to ask instead what this enjoyment is doing for us or to us, and we can see why David Cameron might need this type of distracting enjoyment to make his working life appear (to himself) as productive and important. Whilst the hope of the politician is that a shared enjoyment with the voter will garner votes, it's in fact rather worrying that Angry Birds is a necessary supplement to the most powerful job in the country.

For Walter Benjamin, distraction is not simply a matter of a deficit of attention which distracts from an otherwise stable reality, but instead implies a scattering or dispersion, which he sees as constitutive of modern mass culture. Anticipating Jean Baudrillard and his analysis of postmodern culture that was to come years later, Benjamin explains how the individual is bombarded with signs so that no coherent reality can be found; the individual self and its reality become fragmented and scattered because there is so much distraction that there is no normality left to be distracted from.[35] This surely goes some way to explaining the functioning of Candy Crush Saga. Moments where we feel distracted now have another purpose, that of implying that there is, outside our distraction, a coherent reality which we can and should tap back into as and when we please or feel obliged. This also makes sense in light of how often we turn to our phones, to Buzzfeed or to Candy Crush, precisely when we feel most alienated and dissatisfied with our work, our thoughts or our lives. In other words, it is self-evident that we don't truly desire to play Candy Crush but unfortunately have to work, but rather that we feel the need for distraction only when we are working, to re-enforce the sense (increasingly lost) that our work has coherent order and value compared to these activities. A few minutes on the website Distractify, and we can return to work and feel like we're doing something. Without the distractions, work satisfaction would massively decrease. Or rather, organized dissatisfaction would likely increase, as people would be forced to increasingly confront their alienation rather than distracting themselves from it.

Commuting home from work by train shows just how often we turn immediately to Candy Crush and distractions like it. On the Manchester-to-Liverpool train line it is not unusual to notice that somewhere near half of the commuters (and a greater percentage of those travelling alone) are engaged in mobile-phone activity. The vast majority of this is what we might call 'distraction entertainment' and ranges from social media and Buzzfeed to mobile-phone gaming. Games such as Candy Crush, Angry Birds, Crossy Road and Temple Run represent a large proportion of this distraction, but the distinction between them is in some cases negligible. The fact that we turn to them after work is telling, and suggests that like the cheeky couple of minutes where we look at Facebook when we should be working on a spreadsheet, they are involved in helping us avoid reflection on the working day.

Whilst some have claimed that Twitter, Buzzfeed and the like embrace a kind of fragmentation compared to the more identity-confirming social-media sites epitomized by Facebook, where identity is carefully mapped and affirmed, we see here that they are two sides of the same coin. Fragmented and distracting enjoyment can often serve to affirm the idea that outside of these moments of nonsensical and mindless distraction is a stable working life and identity to which we can and should return.

Some people post their Candy Crush scores to social media, though this is usually partially ironic, showing that time has been wasted and that the subject is happy with that and wants everyone to know it. For the most part, the enjoyment here depends on hiding the distraction from the big Other. These actions of distraction such as Candy Crush and Buzzfeed or Bored Panda, crucially, are kept away from the prying eyes of bosses at work. This sensation is felt even by those like the present writer, who works in an office of his own and therefore faces no danger of actually being detected. That moment when the user quickly closes the browser window in an instant of realization that they must be seen to return to work, even though there is no possibility of another seeing what they are up to, embodies perfectly the big Other and its instilled sense of social regulation. However, hiding from the big Other does not mean resistance to it or escape from its all-seeing surveillance and exercise of power. Quite the contrary: we want the big Other to see us at these moments, seeking its affirmation. With Walter Benjamin we could say that the distraction provides a falsely comforting sense that the un-distracted work and reality is ordered and productive. With the Lacanian idea of the big Other we can take this further and see that embedded into the distraction is the desire for affirmation from the big Other when we close the game or the browser and return to our productive capitalist employment. The distraction appeals because it simulates a feeling of satisfaction when we 'return to work.'

Case Study 2: Football Manager Handheld

There is another type of distraction going on with a different type of mobile-phone game and a completely different relationship to the big Other is revealed by it. Football Manager is a cultural phenomenon and it would be very difficult to overstate this fact. The game series began in 2005, having developed from the Championship Manager series immensely popular in the 1990s. It has grown steadily since then into what it is today, a game that has been cited as a contributing factor in dozens of divorce cases, has been the subject of two films, has had a book written about its ability to ruin lives, and has become one of the fastest-selling PC games of all time. The game has bizarrely even had an influence on the real football world that it simulates. In 2008, Everton FC signed a deal with the game manufacturer Sports Interactive which allowed them to use the game's database to scout players and opposition. On November 2012, Azerbaijani student Vugar Huseynzade was promoted to the manager of FC Baku's reserve team, a club in the top division of Azerbaijani football, based on his success in Football Manager.[36] The line between simulation and reality in this game is, in a very real way, a fine one.

The remarkable book *Football Manager Stole My Life* amazes the reader on every page with its accounts of how the game has provided enjoyment to people across the world, with stories from celebrities preferring their in-game life to their glamorous careers to those who marriages have been threatened and even broken by addiction to the game, or even by particular events within the game that have driven the player to near insanity.[37] This shows already how different this enjoyment is to that of Candy Crush, which might be slightly frustrating but is based on distraction rather than investment.

The writer here is a dedicated player of the game who replays his imaginary press conferences in his head on the way to work. In this respect, this section ought to recognize that it hopes to share something with the approach of Roland Barthes' *Mythologies*, in which the analyses of everyday phenomena come from the perspective of someone deeply entrenched within those structures. Barthes refreshingly writes about the Tour de France and amateur wrestling from the perspective of someone who has very much enjoyed those things, avoiding a tendency still too prevalent in academia to criticize what the writer doesn't like and to praise what they do.[38] While the criticism can be made that the resulting discussion will be biased as it comes from the perspective of someone who has been subjected to ideology of the enjoyment in question, discussing moments of enjoyment that have been experienced can involve insight into the effects of these enjoyments on the subjectivity in question. Writing on what we enjoy and especially on what we enjoy but cannot always explain why we are enjoying should at least attempt to involve discovering something about the way our enjoyment is structured that was previously unknown to us as enjoying subjects.

Those who have played the game for any significant period

will be familiar with a feeling of having wasted time when the game is lost or a season goes badly. This strangely contrasts with a feeling of productivity felt when Football Manager goes well and the game is 'won.' There is in fact no way to win the game, which can be played endlessly. We might link this guilt after playing to the idea of punishing our infidelity to our 'real lives' in order to re-establish those 'productive' lives as important. Yet, the fact that this feeling only happens when our fate in the game itself is met with failure suggests that there is more to the ideology of Football Manager than just that.

Just as Candy Crush is representative of other, similar mobile-phone games, there are other games that share with Football Manager this increased hold over the subject. Games such as *Civilization* and *World of Warcraft* produce similar feelings in their users. Football Manager though, does seem to be the epitome of a certain type of investment demanded by the gamer. Avid players of the game I interviewed for this book made the following comments, which should give a sense of the power of the game over its users:

It allows me to live my dream job. It combines my passion and knowledge in one of the world's toughest places to be successful.

There have been days (more often than I'd like to admit) when I have given more to my FM life than to my real life. But that's how you win the Champions League with Lille.

I genuinely think of myself as an FM expert these days. I certainly got hooked because lots of people played it. Running home from school to get us all set up. Agreeing the fairest teams to each of our abilities and then testing our knowledge and skill against each other. But once we were adults finding time when we were all free was hard to do, at which point it became about playing on your own and bettering yourself.

It fills up every second. I even play it while I walk home

from the shops with all the grocery bags making my other hand hurt so I can keep one hand free for Football Manager Handheld.

The statements suggest a number of things. Firstly, that the appeal of the game is connected to work and the idea of a 'dream job' that is presumably opposed to the jobs actually held by those playing the game. Second, they suggest that these games do more than distract from those 'real' jobs but create a kind of alternative universe in which to experience simulated 'success,' as with the comparison between 'FM life' and 'real life.' Another interviewee commented that Football Manager makes them feel 'invincible,' confessing: 'if I lose I can simply re-start my device.' This language of simulated successful careers points to a relationship between the game and work, and suggests that it may involve distraction from dissatisfaction in the user's 'real life.' Like Candy Crush, in which the user can post their scores to social media and thus compete with peers, Football Manager sucks people in through competition with others, but then continues long after the other has disappeared in the isolated and imaginary world of the very much individual player. By 2014, with the advent of Football Manager Handheld, which does not have a multiplayer function, the user competes only with imaginary 'others.' All these statements help uncover what Football Manager is all about.

The replacement of the actual other with whom the subject competes (say, a fellow FM gamer from school) with an imaginary or virtual other (the computer AI) offers a way of bringing Freudian psychoanalysis to bear on the modern state. The vast majority of video games work in this way at least to some degree, suggesting a greater relevance to our entertainment than just Football Manager. In one of his most ground-breaking essays, 'Beyond the Pleasure Principle,' Freud discusses the pleasure found in children's games and writes:

If the doctor looks down a child's throat or carries out some small operation on him, we may be quite sure that these frightening experiences will be the subject of the next game; but we must not in that connection overlook the fact that there is a yield of pleasure from another source. As the child passes over from the passivity of the experience to the activity of the game, he hands on the disagreeable experience to one of his playmates and in this way revenges himself on a substitute.[39]

The statement makes something clearer about the relationship between Football Manager and the workplace that was suggested by the statements from those interviewed about their enjoyment of the game. The child's experience at the doctor's must be seen as analogous to the employee's feelings in the workplace, being passively operated on whilst a figure of authority commands conformity. The school room may be thought of as a more appropriate analogy, and indeed those interviewed about Football Manager felt that a key point was that their enjoyment of the game began in their school days. After making this fairly speculative jump, a smaller jump can easily be made to see how the appeal of playing Football Manager with friends came as a result of school. Just as those in the workplace immediately shun their jobs to get out their phones and play distracting games on the train home, those interviewed recount 'running home from school' to start Football Manager with their peers.

One interviewee accounted for their playing the game by discussing the 'passion and knowledge' required to 'be successful' in a 'tough' environment in the game. Another saw the appeal as directly connected to their peers 'testing our knowledge and skill against each other.' Passion, knowledge and skill all seem to be part of the ideology of the school and of the workplace. In Freud's terms from the quotation above, the subject, having suffered at the hands of power at work, derives 'a yield of pleasure from another source' by passing over from 'the passivity of the experience' to 'the activity of the game,' becoming, in the experience of Football Manager, an active player who can subject the other to a substituted version of what he has himself been subjected to. The competition amongst friends and the desire to be seen as an 'expert' of the game seem to match exactly with Freud's point that the subject 'hands on the disagreeable experience to one of his playmates and in this way revenges himself on a substitute.' The possibility of victory over the 'playmate' produces the potential pleasure that would revenge the subject's school and/or work defeat. This would also explain why the sensation of having wasted time is only applicable when the subject loses the game. In this case, the game has not served its purpose.

One interviewee also noticed how the game moves from a social to an individual level, and this brings Freud's comments into the 21st century. Claiming that 'once we were adults [...] it became about playing on your own and bettering yourself,' the interviewee shows us that this concrete other is replaced by an imaginary one. The defeat of the computer in the game, or an improvement on your past attempt to defeat the computer, only works because of the imaginary other who can be defeated and the imaginary big Other who can see and approve this defeat. Whilst Candy Crush largely works by hiding from the big Other and feeling that we have not been seen playing, here the game is structured on imaginary approval for the player's success and the skills and knowledge demonstrated by the player's achievements. A quick look online reveals thousands of Football Manager blogs where players share their successes with the internet and experience a sense of public approval, but even the private player clearly imagines something similar...

What we see in Football Manager is the replacement of the real playmate with a virtual one. This also explains why it was necessary for Football Manager to move to the handheld mobile-phone format in 2014: so that revenge against this imaginary virtual playmate could be taken immediately after work for any injustices done there throughout the day. The process wouldn't work as effectively if you had to return home and arrange a game with your friends to take out your frustrations on each other (you might have time on the train home to reflect on your working conditions), and in any case, if you did that you couldn't *all* win. Alienated in the workplace, we turn to a simulated feeling of career satisfaction which works to re-enforce the criteria we use to judge 'success,' only serving to exacerbate our sense of having more to achieve by creating an ideal of career success towards which we feel we should strive. The game operates like Candy Crush, to prevent us facing our dissatisfaction and thinking about it (which could at least potentially lead to organized opposition and revolt). Yet, at the same time it operates on us in another way, instilling a sense of career 'success' which builds up our desire to strive towards this capitalist ideal. After we finish chastising ourselves for playing the game (and for taking time off from being productive in our jobs to do so), we return to work not only having managed to avoid confronting our dissatisfaction but with our sense of commitment to capitalist success very much renewed.

3. Irrational Enjoyment: *Jouissance* and Enjoyment Studies

> The everyday escapes. Why does it escape? Because it is without a subject. When I live the everyday, it is anyone, anyone whatsoever, who does so.
> – Maurice Blanchot[40]

Over the last twenty or so years the genealogy of cultural studies has changed and the study of 'popular culture' has become an increasingly prominent feature of university courses.[41] Many universities began offering courses on 'popular culture' following on from a boom in 'contemporary literature,' 'contemporary film' and 'contemporary art' courses. This boom in 'popular culture studies' has meant that we are talking about what we enjoy, and what others enjoy, much more frequently in the university than ever before.

Today, there are not only a great many modules on 'popular culture,' but a first-year university course in an arts-based subject such as English Literature is likely to include a section on 'popular culture,' often tacked on to the end of a compulsory 'introduction to literature' course which all students study, whether they have chosen to or not. This may be an important point because it suggests that we are now teaching students how to relate to the popular as standard, placing a new level of responsibility on the university as it teaches a new generation of academics, journalists and teachers how they ought to think about popular and everyday life, and how to think about their own enjoyment and that of others. It is essential to explore the effect of this change on the university and on our enjoyment, and especially on the relationship between the two. The media (another equally complex discourse) has had much to say on the matter. There has been much criticism, skepticism, and occasionally backing, of seemingly 'unusual' course modules such as 'Beyoncé Studies,' 'Jedi Studies,' 'Ghost Hunting' and 'David Beckham Studies.' What we really need, I hope to have suggested throughout this book, is a new kind of degree in 'Enjoyment Studies.'

Even from personal experience in the teaching of English Literature, over the course of the last ten years it has become apparent that there has been a definite shift in the status of 'popular culture' in the university. Whilst 'the popular' has been a 'topic' since the start of that time and indeed before, it has now become an 'assumed' part of literary and cultural studies. Media debate seems to have centered on whether this is 'right' or not, and has considered whether it is a legitimate topic when compared to studies of the literary canon or even contemporary art and literature by 'legitimate' authors or artists. In other words, it has asked whether a study of Justin Bieber can be compared to or even replace a seminar on John Milton. This is not a question I will be involved in answering here. Instead I will think about what it means that the university has changed its attitude to what it deems to be 'the popular' and to enjoyment. Ultimately what all this demonstrates is the score of the project of rationalizing enjoyment in our culture and the university's key role within it.

In his 17th seminar, called *The Other Side of Psychoanalysis,* Lacan outlines what he calls the 'four discourses.' He describes four major discourses (though there is a suggestion of a fifth, the capitalist discourse, in his later work). Each can be thought of as a type of structure that we can identify in the way particular parts of our society are organized. Lacan's schemata of the four discourses have been more or less accurately summarized (as far as is possible) by Tony Brown and his collaborators as: (1) systems of knowledge (the university discourse); (2) discourses of control or governance (the master's discourse); (3) the alienated or divided subject split between alternative discursive modes (this is the discourse of the hysteric and I won't be saying much about this here); and (4) systematic resistance to oppressive power structures (the analytic discourse).[42] These, in the briefest summary, are Lacan's four discourses. All of these operate at the same time and in different contexts they can overlap and become confused. It is not the case, for instance, that a hysteric will always be operating through the hysteric's discourse. Not everything the university does is in the structure of the university discourse, and the analyst is not always acting in accordance with the analyst's discourse, etc, etc.

We can use this schema to explain what is going on in the relationship between the university and enjoyment. What we ultimately see is that studies of enjoyment have increasingly become a part of number 1 on this schema: the university discourse. The university is not acting alone here and should be seen as something more like the embodiment of the major ideological trends that are organizing our social structure at the moment. The approach really needed to discuss enjoyment is number 4: the analyst's discourse, as I shall show later in the chapter with my examples of 'irrational enjoyment.' This argument would traditionally meet with some resistance, as it involves seeing popular enjoyment as part of a resistance to oppressive power structures.

Academic discourse has often seen popular culture as the arm of the state (the master's discourse in the schema above). Theodor Adorno for instance, would come into this category. It is common for Adorno to be the first 'theorist' taught on university degree courses in the UK – pointing students into a particular idea of the relationship between theory and popular culture. Lacan on the other hand is often the last 'theorist' an undergraduate comes into contact with, providing they have remained open-minded enough to have waded through the countless suggestions of his inapplicability and backwardness offered to students by lecturers who dismiss Lacan to students without asking them to read a word of his seminars first. Adorno's conversations with popular culture are immensely interesting and varied but have largely been used by the university as evidence for seeing things that are popular as the arm of the master's discourse.[43] This would make the popular unsuitable for the analyst's discourse, which as we have seen is 'systematic resistance to oppressive power structures.'

For Lacan, in the 'master's discourse,' the discourse most associated with governance and control, all knowledge works in the service of 'the master'. The master might be thought of as the order of things or the state of power relations in a given time and place. The position of this master cannot be questioned. One example of the master would be a 'king,' who is king not because there was a discussion about whether or not there should be a king in the first place or who should be elected to be king, but because he *is* that thing: it is just there. In our society the master would be somewhat more complex, but perhaps not as different as we imagine. This position of power operates on 'knowledge' and makes all knowledge (we could use the word 'ideology' in place of knowledge) *work for it*, so that all knowledge and ideology works in the service of the master. Knowledge is made to justify the master's position and further entrench it, guaranteeing that it remains in place.

When the organization of discourse moves into what Lacan calls the 'university discourse,' knowledge moves from being the servant of the master to being the master itself. In the university, knowledge has the most privileged position; it is placed on a pedestal and it cannot be moved. We can think of the university's pursuit of 'truth' in this way: the truth is just there and there is nothing we can do to change the 'truth,' we must just continually work towards it. In the 'master's discourse' it was knowledge that worked for the master like a slave, entrenching it and guaranteeing its hold. But now, in the university discourse, knowledge is occupying the master's role. So what, for Lacan, would fill the role left empty by knowledge? The answer he proposes is: enjoyment.

What happens in the university then is this: knowledge controls or has a power over enjoyment. In other words, the university makes enjoyment (often unexplainable enjoyment) work for it, just as the master's discourse made knowledge work for *it*self. This puts the university in a different kind of position when it comes to the popular. It reverses the idea that 'the popular' (the university's language) works in the service of the master and the universities' job is to show how problematic these enjoyments are. Instead, the university's effort to explain how enjoyment works is in the service of the very master it thinks it is attacking. At a stretch we could go back to the language of the quotation above and put it something like this: knowledge, supported by forces of order and governance, operates a power over enjoyment that is potentially resistant to oppressive power structures. This is what we might say is involved in the university's treatment of popular culture: speaking for it and pulling it onto its own side by explaining the enjoyment experienced there in its own terms. In other words, the university uses the popular to show that its knowledge is true. It operates a power over enjoyment so that enjoyment seems to entrench and guarantee that the knowledge of the university is correct and remains privileged and embedded.

Even the language of some of the 'popular culture' course outlines found in the university today provide clear evidence of this happening. There are a couple of examples that make this immediately clear. One course on Beyoncé Studies, for instance, claims that it 'will use Beyoncé's career as a jumping off point to explore American race, gender and sexual politics.' This implies that any number of texts or individuals could have provided this 'spring board' to introduce issues such as race and gender that are already present in academic theory anyway. It borrows an approach common in the university of looking at the Theory or

Idea of X through the Text of Y. The Y is interchangeable and Beyoncé can be used to introduce or explain X just as well as Virginia Woolf. The gesture made here is: 'look, our academic ideas also explain popular things you like and enjoy as well as just old books.' Crucially, whilst applying them to 'new' things, it leaves academic structures intact.

Another contemporary course that discusses pop music and sports puts it this way in its list of aims:

> The course explores how gender, class, ethnicity, and race define and shape contemporary societies and our everyday lives.
>
> WNBA v. NBA? How does gender shape our understanding of sports?[44]

Even here the bias is implicit. It is as if already existing and *constant* structures of gender, class, race etc. explain and shape contemporary societies and everyday lives. The course asks how existing ideas of gender affect sports, but not how sports affect existing ideas of gender. These courses might explore how Beyoncé shows us the truth of an idea developed in gender studies, but they seem unlikely to see popular culture and everyday enjoyment as something itself challenging and transformative to our social world.

There is evidence that this 'university discourse' is by no means confined to the university itself, a point Lacan makes clear too. Much of the media seems to function with the logic of the university. A 2015 article in *The Guardian* featured seven philosophers or philosophy lecturers discussing a chosen philosophical idea in relation to a film. Whilst the philosophers, in most cases, were not particularly guilty of simply using the chosen film to prove an already existing point (though some were bordering on it), the title of the article was: 'I watch therefore I am: seven movies that teach us key philosophical lessons.'[45] The choice of title shows the acceptance of a certain relationship between philosophy and the world around it, a relationship that is one-way: the films reflect and prove philosophical ideas, allowing them to retain their status and relevance but without insisting those ideas are themselves changed and challenged.

This book has been about the regulation and rationalization of enjoyment, and it has shown how the more culturally acceptable enjoyment of high-brow literature and apparently 'irrational' or 'useless' enjoyment of mobile-phone games in fact work side-by-side to organize our pleasure. In a way, both can be seen as the arm of the master's discourse. Neither, then, can be described as 'resistance to oppressive power struggles,' but there may be another alternative, an enjoyment that serves a more radical purpose.

In the psychoanalytic concept of '*jouissance*' we might find what we are looking for. For Lacan, *jouissance* is an enjoyment that has no apparent purpose. In English translations of his work the word is usually kept untranslated because whilst it does mean 'enjoyment,' it also suggests a specifically self-destructive kind of sexual enjoyment or compulsion and should be thought of as separate from general ideas of pleasure. *Jouissance* is enjoyment that we cannot quite see, imagine, or measure the value of. There is no more accurate summary of this complex concept of *jouissance* than that given by Dylan Evans:

> It is only in 1960 that Lacan develops his classic opposition between *jouissance* and pleasure, an opposition which alludes to the Hegelian/Kojevian distinction between enjoyment and pleasure. The pleasure principle functions as a limit to enjoyment; it is a law which commands the subject to 'enjoy as little as possible.' At the same time the subject constantly attempts to transgress the prohibitions imposed on his enjoyment, to go 'beyond the pleasure principle.' However, the result of transgressing the pleasure principle is not more

pleasure but pain, since there is only a certain amount of pleasure that the subject can bear. Beyond this limit, pleasure becomes pain, and this 'painful pleasure' is what Lacan calls *jouissance; 'jouissance* is suffering.'[46]

Jouissance then, is pleasure, but it is also opposed to pleasure, making it something different to the enjoyments that we are constantly commanded to experience in our culture today. As Evans goes on to explain, on entry into the symbolic order the subject has to renounce this *jouissance*. The symbolic order of culture is best thought of as the language and ideology in which we are contained. This connects to the discussion in the introduction of the way that society traditionally works to prohibit enjoyment but now appears to insist upon it. Lacan's distinction between other forms of enjoyment and pleasure on the one hand and *jouissance* on the other may help us to think through this change. Whilst some forms of pleasure are compulsory and demanded, we can ask whether there is not still a type of enjoyment that is more transgressive and radical. For Lacan, since *jouissance* always involves transgressing a prohibition imposed by the pleasure principle, we can say that it is 'always transgressive.' He writes that '*jouissance* is forbidden to him who speaks, as such.'[47] Whilst we live in a society in which 'god demands a *constant state of enjoyment*,' we do not live in a society that embraces Lacanian *jouissance*. On the contrary, it is forbidden.

When I discuss 'Gangnam Style,' twerking and *Game of Thrones* below, I am not claiming that these are things that we are forbidden to enjoy. Of course, they are examples of the enjoyment on offer in our capitalist order that commands constant enjoyment, and they are examples of enjoyment regularly posted to social media to score points in the competition to enjoy the most. It is rather that, in our enjoyment of these varied and diverse things, we can or might experience moments of *jouissance* which trouble the structure of the capitalist subject. I use these examples to make some of these moments of *jouissance* visible, but it is equally possible for these peculiar instances of enjoyment to erupt into any of the activities discussed above, or any other form of enjoyment. In other words, this is not about whether 'Gangnam Style' is more radical than Football Manager, even if the present writer suspects this might be the case. When we experience moments of *jouissance* we tend to ignore them and discount their importance, or try to explain them as the university does by exercising a power over these moments and 'rationalizing' them. In fact, there is something much more irrational and inexplicable about them in which we can find an enjoyment that is, at least in some way, a 'resistance to oppressive power structures.'

The two case studies below offer an alternative to discussing enjoyment as the 'university discourse' would: pulling it onto its side and proving its existing knowledge to be correct. In another discourse, the 'analyst's discourse (for Lacan the most desirable of the four), there is a different agenda. As discussed above, in the master discourse the order of things is in what we might call the 'position of privilege,' and in the university discourse knowledge is placed in the position of privilege. In each of these, the master and knowledge are in the 'driving seat,' having a power over the other things in the discourse: the master has a power over knowledge and knowledge has a power over enjoyment. In the fourth discourse, the analyst's discourse, it is enjoyment (or *jouissance*) that is placed in the position of privilege. This means putting enjoyment first and recognizing that it plays a key role in constructing us and our social relations. In the analyst's discourse enjoyment operates on the subject and makes the subject work for it. In other words, this model recognizes that enjoyment is not just a reflection of who we are and how we are constructed but a key tool in our construction. The following two case studies attempt to treat enjoyment in this way, recognizing that enjoyment is a powerful force that constructs the subject and looking for the difficult to explain moments of enjoyment that have an effect on us and determine us in ways that we don't already understand. This way of approaching enjoyment hopes to make new parts of our ideology visible rather than just affirming already-existing knowledge.

The previous two chapters have identified two organized forms of enjoyment that are counterparts to each other. What follows here is a discussion of an enjoyment that *shows us how we are constructed* rather than enjoyment that escapes or attempts to escape these constructions. It is not, then, an extreme or radical enjoyment to be positively invested in as 'free' of social constraint, nor a moment of (even temporary) liberation from oppressive power structures. Rather, it is a moment that can point out to us how we are constructed and how some of the ideological structures of our experience are put together. In other words, the radicalism of this enjoyment is not found in its escaping the regulation and organization of enjoyment that has been discussed in this book so far. Rather, its radicalism is in revealing this to us; it is an enjoyment that shows us how we are organized.

Case Study 1: 'Gangnam Style' and Twerking

As we discussed in our introduction to the second Everyday Analysis book, *Twerking to Twerking*, Slavoj Žižek has made a vital analysis of the Korean pop sensation Psy's 'Gangnam Style' and how it works on us.[48] He writes:

> 'Gangnam Style' is not ideology in spite of ironic distance, it is ideology because of it: [...] the self-mocking irony of 'Gangnam Style' makes palpable the stupid enjoyment of the rave music. Many listeners find the song disgustingly attractive, i.e., they 'love to hate it', or, rather, they enjoy the very fact of finding it disgusting so they repeatedly play it to

prolong their disgust. Such an ecstatic surrender to obscene *jouissance* in all its stupidity entangles the subject into what Lacan, following Freud, calls 'drive'; perhaps its paradigmatic expressions are the repulsive private rituals (sniffing one's own sweat, sticking one's finger into one's nose, etc.) that bring intense satisfaction without our being aware of it – or, insofar as we are aware of it, without our being able to do anything to prevent it.[49]

Here Žižek suggests that in our enjoyment of Psy's 'Gangnam Style' there is something that goes beyond what we can explain, which does not seem 'enjoyable' at all but which nonetheless produces in us a strange and intense satisfaction. This is also visible in the phenomenon of 'twerking,' something that now needs no introduction. Whilst the movements involved in a twerk are certainly *suggestive*, it is difficult to pinpoint exactly of what they are suggestive; and whilst this suggestiveness (and *suggestiveness* in general) is no doubt sexual, in the actual act of sex it would again be difficult to correlatively place this maneuver (too fast to be a sensual 'grind,' too erratic to be a portrayal of copulation). As an ecstatic movement, it seems to derive enjoyment in those doing it from the 'motor' drive (of bodily movement) and in those watching from the 'scopic' drive (of the probably male gaze). Immediate parallels are apparent between Žižek's discussion of 'Gangnam Style' and this reading of twerking. Both can be seen as 'the stupid enjoyment' and both might make the subject enjoying wonder whether they 'enjoy the very fact of finding it disgusting.' Without much of a stretch it could also be connected to the enjoyment of disgusting drives such as 'sniffing one's own sweat, sticking one's finger into one's nose, etc.' and other forms of pleasure/pain in which we cannot really explain or quantify the levels of pleasure involved.

This also links to the Lacanian idea of *jouissance*. These moments could be seen as 'painful pleasure' and even as 'suffering,' as anyone who's been made to watch the full video of 'Gangnam Style' is likely to have found. It may also suggest Lacan's sense that 'that there is only a certain amount of pleasure that the subject can bear.' These excessive gestures and enjoyments clearly exceed what we are comfortable with.

Does this enjoyment, this *jouissance*, still work in the service of governance and control? In some cases it is easy to see how it could still benefit the capitalist insistence on enjoyment, for instance with the huge money-making industry of 'Gangnam Style,' the most 'liked' video on YouTube, and with the culture of the 'twerk,' a profitable tool to sell media and advertising space. Both twerking and 'Gangnam Style' also have a certain 'orientalism' to them, a term coined by Edward Said to describe the West's representation and consumption of the East.[50] Twerking, which copies or perhaps develops a West-African and later African-American dance style, has both gendered and racialized connotations and may involve a kind of Western and patriarchal fetishizing of the female other of a kind that has been discussed by much postcolonial theory. Less obviously, 'Gangnam Style' is also involved the Western consumption of a caricatured Eastern culture, though there are many levels to this since the song is already coded as a representation of an 'other' in Korean culture itself, as I shall discuss further. But the ideological structures behind these moments are often invisible to us. Seeing the moment as *jouissance* does not mean seeing it as anything other than ideological. It does not mean that there are not ideological reasons for the enjoyment. Rather, the inexplicable yield of pleasure from the moment is deeply rooted in ideological structures, just as it is when we experience strange enjoyment when biting our nails or picking our toes. Seeing the moment as *jouissance* means looking at the way it operates on us and forms us ideologically through our pleasure, but the pleasure also exceeds what we can explain, pointing to the gaps in ideology itself and the fact that we are constructed as incomplete subjects, something capitalism would like to hide.

'Gangnam Style' needs a closer look than Žižek gives it. The phrase 'Gangnam Style' is a Korean neologism that refers to a lifestyle associated with the Gangnam District of Seoul, where people are considered to be trendy, hip and to exude a certain supposed 'class.' In other words, the recreation and enjoyment taking place in the Gangnam District, at least from Psy's perspective, is the embodiment of the 'rational,' coming with cultural capital and signifying an idea of culture that fits Bourdieu's model perfectly: those involved see themselves as having the gift of nature to enjoy certain things. The last thing they would enjoy is 'Gangnam Style.' When interviewed in some Korean publications Psy has shown an intense awareness of what he is doing in the song and even of its political position. Interviewed in *Time* magazine, however, when asked what 'Gangnam Style' was all about, Psy replied:

> Honestly, it's to the ladies, to the classy ladies, you know. I want them going crazy, and especially just for me. We all want that.[51]

Psy's reply seems to be in the style of those trendy characters mocked in his video. It points to our inability to rationalize the actions of the video but also mocks our own need to work it out and explain it. It seems to almost directly mock the course outlines quoted above which attempt to see popular culture as a straightforward 'reflection' of pre-existing and stable cultural ideas.

Psy claims here that his actions when dancing are entirely self-interested, when in fact we know that they are anything but his 'natural' style and that the enjoyment found in the dancing comes from an abandonment of his own individuality and a launching into 'style' constructed by another culture. McGowan discusses this as an idea at the heart of psychoanalysis that is often misread and misunderstood by critics of both Freud and Lacan. Discussing these criticisms as embodied by the critique of psychoanalysis offered by John Farrell, McGowan writes:

> John Farrell claims that under the spell of psychoanalysis 'every appearance of good must be exposed as unconscious hypocrisy, every commitment to public interests and to social institutions must be recognized for what it is—a disguise for narcissistic gratification or a painful instinctual concession.' Farrell, like so many critics of psychoanalysis, sees Freud as a prophet of human selfishness. But this attack on psychoanalysis— perhaps the most popular of all attacks— completely misunderstands what is at stake in psychoanalytic interpretation. Rather than uncovering narcissistic self-interest behind a benevolent act, Freud uncovers the abandonment of self-interest that is at stake behind a seemingly self-interested act.[52]

This, quite strangely, explains 'Gangnam Style.' Whilst we might be hard-pressed to describe Psy's song and the accompanying video as a 'benevolent act,' we can see based on the discussion here that it is an act of parody and of social critique, showing up the arrogance and pretense of the culture in the Gangnam district (and with it, perhaps accounting for a little bit of its UK success, the Hipster culture so prevalent in, say, Shoreditch). If Farrell was right about psychoanalysis (which he isn't), this apparently legitimate social critique could be uncovered as 'a disguise for narcissistic gratification.' But it is in fact as if Psy already knows this and mocks it when he says 'honestly, it's to the ladies, to the classy ladies, you know. I want them going crazy, and especially just for me.' Instead, applying a more genuine psychoanalytic approach makes more sense and it can easily be seen that in another way Psy's performance 'uncovers the abandonment of self-interest that is at stake behind a seemingly self-interested act.' The fact that Psy is a major Korean pop-star with a history of celebrating his own celebrity status makes the release of his song 'a seemingly self-interested act,' but the video involves an abandonment of individuality. Psychoanalysis shows how when we seem to be acting for ourselves we are often abandoning any agency and acting instead in the service of our social discourse, the big Other, or in the service of 'the master' more generally. Psy's performance and our enjoyment of it involve a strange 'giving up' of unique identity and an abandonment to the completely pre-subscribed cultural identities dished to the subjects of the Gangnam District. In other words, everything in 'Gangnam Style' is a copy, with nothing individualist about it. It can also be seen that the Hipster culture it mocks is one in which everything is a copy, and also that the enjoyment of the song involves the enjoyment of copying (for instance the number of YouTube copies of people doing the Gangnam Style dance). Psy's name, a shortened form of psytrance, suggests a whole identity built on mimicry. There is something similar and copy-like about other enjoyments too, with twerking another example of an infinitely copied gesture that produces pleasure. Yet another recent cultural phenomenon to fit this model is the 'Harlem Shake,' and the complete list would probably be endless.

The epigraph to this chapter is Maurice Blanchot's statement:

The everyday escapes. Why does it escape? Because it is without a subject. When I live the everyday, it is anyone, anyone whatsoever, who does so.[53]

These moments are 'everyday' in that they are enjoyment that fits this description, and of course in that they happen every day. There is, in a way, a loss of identity in these moments. However, it would be better to characterize this not as a loss of identity or an escape from the identities imposed upon us by capitalism but as an abandonment of oneself to the completely constructed nature of identity. In the enjoyment of an extreme copying taken to mad and excessive levels, it can be seen how *jouissance* works: it is a moment of *everyday enjoyment* which is completely ideological and which constructs identity but appears to be mindless and innocent, which does not make rational sense in the smooth functioning of capitalism since it involves forgoing an individualism upon which those structures are dependent. In other words, 'Gangnam Style' as a moment of *jouissance* shows us that we are not unique subjects with unique enjoyments but subjects whose enjoyment forms us in accordance with a set of rules – and that there is therefore no 'gift of nature' to what we enjoy at all.

Case Study 2: *Game of Thrones*, Brueghel and Bosch

Game of Thrones is an important choice of case study for this chapter because it has been discussed by what we might call the 'university discourse.' The *Blackwell Philosophy and Pop Culture Series* unsurprisingly includes a book called *Game of Thrones and Philosophy*. The series has produced dozens of such books, each of which combines a popular television show (from *South Park* and *The Office* to *24* and *Mad Men*) with a history of philosophy. The books have been produced with incredible speed over a very short period of the last five years, perhaps indicating just how easy the authors have found their task. The book is a perfect example of the 'university discourse' discussed in the first half of this chapter (despite the fact that we can easily imagine the sniggers that the university professor is likely to make at such a book). The text routinely and repeatedly uses the primary text (in this case both the novels and TV series of *Game of Thrones*) to prove correct long-standing academic theory and philosophy. We read, for example:

> According to Foucault, knowledge of insanity has depended upon those with power to name it, whose power in turn

increased with their ability to designate certain people as insane. For example, both Stannis Baratheon and Joffrey Lannister surround themselves with entertainers known as mad fools.[54]

The passage here, when taken out of context, appears almost to be a joke about theory and its misapplications, proving Foucault is right on the grounds that a fictional king calls his entertainer a nutcase in a popular TV show. However, it is in fact a relatively fair passage to embody the approach the book takes. At every turn (or at least most turns, since a few essays in the volume don't deserve the criticism), it explains how philosophical ideas are borne out in the text, thus proving them to be at least valid if not entirely correct. The dual project seems to be firstly to show how interesting *Game of Thrones* is by looking at how it deals with so many major philosophical issues, and secondly to show how exciting philosophy can be when we realize it can be joined up with our favorite fun and engaging television series. The book enticingly asks:

What would Hobbes think about the political situation in Westeros? How would he advise the nobility of the great houses? What makes the perspective of Thomas Hobbes so fascinating is that he lived through the game of thrones *for real*. [...] The Stuarts reigned over England (once seven kingdoms itself!). [...] Like the Targaryens, their house was overthrown by their subjects in a terrible civil war.[55]

This approach is completely problematic and it works to avoid saying anything new about philosophy. In his important book on Jacques Lacan, psychoanalytic theorist Jean-Claude Milner puts it nicely when he writes that:

It is not, therefore, appropriate to present Lacan in a way that would bind it within its own internal logic – consistent or not – and that exposes it completely so that any misinterpretations are corrected. My intention is another entirely: not to clarify Lacan's thoughts, nor to rectify what has been said about it, but to express clearly that there is thought in Lacan's work. Thought, by which I mean something whose existence imposes on those who haven't thought it.[56]

Milner wants to return to Lacan much as Lacan himself returned to Freud, not to develop a totalizing and complete theory but to show how his work reveals problems with or gaps in existing thought. Lacan said of Freud that he was mistakenly read by others 'as one can read anything new [...] pulling it completely to the side of already accepted notions.'[57] Again, this aligns perfectly with the university discourse and its operation to pull enjoyment onto the side of already-accepted notions. Instead, Lacan wanted to revisit Freud in order to see what his work does that cannot be reconciled with existing thought. This is plainly the opposite to the philosophy demonstrated by *Game of Thrones and Philosophy*, a 300-page book which across no less than twenty articles applying theory and philosophy to the show, unsurprisingly makes not one reference to psychoanalysis. This type of reading, if we are to employ Milner's terms, is lacking in 'thought'; it provides nothing new, nothing changing, but simply forces new texts and new moments into the structures that already exist in our language.

Jouissance, then, would be a moment of 'thought,' or at least of potential thought, a moment that insists that the limitations of knowledge are made visible and that new thought is produced to process them. These moments are moments of change, and they structure us as subjects and as a society, but we don't have an existing framework with which to reconcile them. Žižek points out clearly that *jouissance* is not a moment that will never be explained, not an experience that is outside language or knowledge, but a moment that structures us as subjects in ways we are unconscious of. The moment of enjoyable *jouissance* is central to the subject's construction: 'although the subject cannot ever subjectivize it, assume it as its own by way of saying "it is I who want to do this," it nonetheless operates at its very kernel.'[58] *Jouissance* is a peculiar enjoyment which is central to the formation of the subject, but the subject does not grasp the ideology behind it.

In a different context Mark Fisher's book *Capitalist Realism* also points to this function of our society to explain and rationalize that which is central to our construction but not understood by our knowledge. Talking of the work we do in our dreams, Fisher writes:

> If memory disorder provides a compelling analogy for the glitches in capitalist realism, the model for its smooth functioning would be dreamwork. When we are dreaming, we forget, but immediately forget that we have done so, since the gaps and lacunae in our memories are Photoshopped out, they do not trouble or torment us. What dreamwork does is to produce a confabulate consistency which covers over anomalies and contradictions.[59]

In dreams, just as in the particular kind of enjoyment we are calling *jouissance*, there are moments at the very kernel of our identities that structure and construct us but which we repress in the truly Freudian way of forgetting that we have even forgotten. We Photoshop out inconsistencies and lacunae in our enjoyment and cover them up to leave our system of knowledge looking smooth and complete.

How would we read *Game of Thrones* in this way then, looking for the moments of enjoyment that structure us as subjects without Photoshopping out inconsistencies and pulling them onto the side of what we already know about ourselves from theory, philosophy or any other science or discourse?

There are certainly many ways in which we enjoy *Game of Thrones* that we can explain using existing models, many parts of the show and moments of enjoyment when reading the books or watching the series where we respond exactly as we are expected to. In a wonderful recent book which offers a ground-breaking discussion of enjoyment, Robert Pfaller discusses and develops a point made by Žižek a couple of decades ago. Pfaller writes:

> At the beginning of the 1990s, when the art world was dominated by a seemingly omnipresent discourse about 'interactivity,' Slavoj Žižek made an extremely astute comment that was a significant break from the discourse. He maintained that television sitcoms using 'canned laughter' are actually laughing at their own jokes *on behalf of the viewer*.[60]

Žižek's point was that the we are 'relieved of our duty to laugh' in these moments because 'the Other [...] is laughing instead of us.'[61] Pfaller develops the point, suggesting that the importance of this is that we allow our reactions to be carried out by another, essentially pre-subscribing how we react to a situation and making us strangely passive/active by a process that delegates our supposedly most intimate feelings to the other. Pfaller goes on to suggest that these moments show us, in light of Žižek's reading, that 'there are artworks that already contain their own viewing and reception.'[62] It is this point that is vital for a study of enjoyment.

Many parts of our enjoyment of *Game of Thrones* can be explained, and in most cases it would be fairly uninteresting to do so. The violence of the show can be thought of in terms of sadistic voyeurism and likened to a whole history of gory television and film. The overt sexual imagery (more pronounced on television than in the novels) can be thought of as a reflection of carnal desire and a whole history of sexuality and the desire to speak increasingly about sex. The text could probably be made to prove Foucault's *History of Sexuality* to be right.[63] The medievalism of the show would be interesting, and could be thought of with other treatments of our increased interest in the medieval today and our double projection onto the medieval space, which we see simultaneously as a time of tragic violence and ill health on the one hand and romance and liberation on the other. Albeit not in the light of *Game of Thrones*, much academic work has been done on these issues. By contrast, my interest here is in the excess of the enjoyment we experience reading the novels and watching the show, the bits we cannot easily explain as escapism and wish-fulfilment. All these other ways of reading the text conform to Pfaller's idea of an artwork that already contains its own viewing and reception: whether consciously or not, the show uses existing features of our culture to draw us in and make us enjoy, making the show a medley of different forms of enjoyment found and understood elsewhere in society from escapism and voyeurism to sexual wish-fulfilment.

There is, however, and most viewers intuitively agree, an excess present in *Game of Thrones* which leaves us feeling that none or all of the ways we can explain why we enjoy the show are quite enough. This is where *Game of Thrones* shares something important with twerking and 'Gangnam Style.' It is in this unexplainable *jouissance* that the show can be found radical and ideological at the same time. In short, *Game of Thrones* can show us how our enjoyment is involved in constructing subjectivity rather than just reflecting it. It also shows how particularly uncomfortable moments of enjoyment threaten to reveal something of our construction to us.

One of the places where this excess is found is in the bodily. Scenes of excessive flesh and often excessive fat are found more than just sensual and sexual, and indeed they seem at times strangely devoid of producing sexual excitation. There may be something here of Roland Barthes' argument that 'woman is desexualized at the very moment when she is stripped naked.'[64] Barthes' point focused on the appeal of hidden flesh and showed that our desire is for what is always out of sight, whereas in *Game of Thrones* there is something threatening about being confronted with nothing hidden, confusing the viewer as to what is desirable. On account of its visibility, nothing on screen seems enough, confronting us with the structure of our desire, drawing us towards the image but making us want to cover it up at the same time. These scenes walk a boundary between the desirable and the repulsive, making the desirable repulsive and the repulsive desirable.

In this, the experience of watching (and in some cases reading) *Game of Thrones* can be likened to the experience of looking at a painting by Pieter Brueghel the Elder, who lived from around 1525 to 1569. Brueghel's paintings transformed medieval society into a carnival in which identity seems threatened by forcing it to engage with the parts of itself that it would like to repress. His painting *The Fight between Carnival and Lent*, for example, shows subjectivity torn between repression and carnival desire. Hieronymus Bosch, who lived between around 1490 until 1516, was Brueghel's major influence, and the ideas can easily be traced between the two. Bosch's depictions of hell for example, combine the sexual with the painful and sadistic, and also merge the human with the animal, depicting men with the heads of fish and battles between creatures of all types, something that is strangely present in *Game of Thrones*, a text full of humanized animals and animalized humans.

Examples include Bran, who is a 'warg' (an idea from Norse mythology and a coming from the word for 'wolf'), meaning that his mind can move into and control the bodies of animals and perceive the world through their senses. The idea of a warg is also used in *Lord of the Rings* in which they are creatures used by the Orcs for transportation, showing a current cultural fascination with the idea. Other examples from *Game of Thrones* include the character 'the hound,' animalized through his savage nature and unquestioning desire to follow his masters, and the use of ravens, an animal with a whole history of humanization from Edgar Allan Poe through Dickens to Frank Capra's *It's a Wonderful Life*. The most central example might be Daenerys Targaryen giving birth to dragons which she then struggles to mother, an image that might just as well be directly taken from a Bosch painting. Bosch himself is experiencing a strange moment of popularity coinciding with the mass consumption of *Game of Thrones*. Bosch imagery is increasingly popular, evidenced perfectly by Dr. Marten's Heironymus Bosch boots, recently on sale for $140, and matching Bosch 'heaven' and 'hell' satchels fetching $165, as well as other companies producing Bosch wallets, iPhone covers and T-shirts. Perhaps, contrary to general assumption, our enjoyment of Bosch today is not so far removed from our enjoyment of *Game of Thrones*, an enjoyment with a completely different type of cultural capital.

George R. R. Martin's novels have something of a genuine Bosch-like quality to them as well. The sexuality found on screen is often a replacement for sensual and sexual descriptions of eating in the book, and these eating scenes blur the boundary between human and animal flesh and confront the reader with something of a Bosch-like repulsion, leaving the reader confused about the boundaries of human identity. One chapter of the first novel, *A Game of Thrones: Song of Ice and Fire*, for example, opens with the imprisoned Tyrion asked by the guard 'you want eat?' and goes on to blur the description of the guard with that of the food he offers. The guard is 'twenty stone of gross stupidity, with brown rotting teeth' and the language subtly suggests that he is considered the object for consumption rather than the food he offers: 'he was as predictable as he was ugly, but Tyrion *was* hungry.'[65] Though the present book is not one that aims at literary analysis, the *Game of Thrones* novels could be treated to such a study. The suggestion here is that it is often these strange moments of language, rather than the 'gripping' plot or the 'convincing characters' (praise often heard and recounted on the blurbs) that make us enjoy, producing an unexplainable enjoyment when reading the novel which is at least slightly troubling to subjectivity.

Discussing Albert Cook's art criticism in his book *Downcast Eyes*, Martin Jay writes that the artists of Bosch's time were 'overloading the signs in a painting, producing a bewildering excess of apparent referential or symbolic meaning.'[66] Following Cook, he also notes that the next generation of 16th-century artists who developed this tradition 'returned to a more controlled visual repertoire of readable images,' with the sole exception of Brueghel.[67] Rather than seeing the 'postmodern' period as somehow sharing something with the medieval, a point some critics have made, it seems that we are in a period now (perhaps more like the 16th century or a more extreme version of it) in which most art involves a 'controlled visual repertoire of readable images' but in which we occasionally see this 'bewildering excess,' which is more threatening to subjectivity and which is strangely enjoyable though not pleasurable.

The 'themes' of birth imagery, repulsion and attraction, and the divide between human and animal all suggest Julia Kristeva's psychoanalytic conception of the 'abject.' Each of these themes is a sufficient subject for a book of its own, but for this reading the concept of the abject in general is sufficient. For Kristeva, abjection describes a certain kind of repression which involves the subject 'casting off' and banishing parts of its identity felt repulsive in order to establish its identity as something that can be thought of as singular, pure and uncontradictory.[68] The animal must be cast off to constitute the human, the repulsive must be constructed and repelled to constitute the desirable (and especially the legitimately desirable), and the birth must be forgotten and abjected to establish the patriarchal world of masculine independence upon which both the world of *Game of*

Thrones and our own culture are founded. The popularity of *Game of Thrones* and the Bosch industry shows that our moment seems to be distinctive in getting something out of this engagement with the abject and that it may show something particular to contemporary ideology.

Discussing *Game of Thrones* in terms of Kristeva's concept of abjection does not aim to prove Kristeva had a point (though no doubt she did). It is rather that we can see that what we might call a '*jouissance* of abjection' is a process that is *doing something*. Coming into contact with abjection seems to explain some of the excess and inexplicable enjoyment we derive from the show. This does not make the enjoyment found here radical per se. On the contrary, these moments could be read as ones in which the subject comes into contact with a boundary or limit but this contact with the limit can and does work to re-inscribe the limit itself. Certain moments of enjoyment experienced by the viewer and reader of *Game of Thrones* are in coming into contact with these pleasure/pain, attraction/repulsion divides which are no doubt found 'enjoyable' even if they cannot be said to be pleasurable or desirable.

This enjoyment is not positive or negative, neither on the side of pain nor pleasure, even though a history of discussing enjoyment has seen it as inherently positive (see the discussion of Bentham in the conclusion). The enjoyment is *jouissance*, a formational moment of subjectivity that may well be completely ideological but which the subject cannot explain using the conscious ideologies it has at its disposal. The moment when the subject is confronted with a blurring between animal and human operates on the subject, forcing it to carry out something like Fisher's 'dreamwork' on the experience, dividing repulsion from attraction and forming this divide in the subject's consciousness at the very moment it seems to be threatened. Perhaps the enjoyment of a mythical medievalism characterized by Bosch and *Game of Thrones* involves recognizing that these divides between attraction and repulsion and enjoyment and displeasure are all too secure in our current moment, and projecting back onto a mythical-medieval space the idea of a subject more liberated from the divides imposed on our unconscious today.

On the other hand, there is a way in which this re-engaging with the abject, this enjoyment that confronts the subject with a divide in its consciousness and asks the subject to see (or at least experience in an unsettling way) this divide happening, can be a more radical way not necessarily of enjoying but of discussing enjoyment. An approach that looks for these formational moments of *jouissance*, which show us how the subject is constructed, seeks to avoid explaining and rationalizing these moments so that capitalism can continue to function smoothly. Instead, it aims to point to these moments of enjoyment which result from deeply rooted structures of our subjectivity and which form the subject in accordance with the ideological demands of its moment. In other words, *jouissance* is completely ideological and makes no claims to being an enjoyment that goes beyond the structure of our ideology. However, these moments show us how ideology operates underneath what we can articulate and how we are formed as subjects as a result of often inexplicable yet ideological moments of enjoyment.

It also shows that our knowledge, which attempts to explain all or at least to have the potential to explain all, is always structure by gaps, lacunae and inconsistencies that show we are by no means in complete control or in knowledge of our own ideology. This enjoyment, albeit a part of our ideology, 'escapes,' as Blanchot puts it, resisting the rationality of the system into which it erupts and showing us something that the system would like to keep hidden. This enjoyment can be thought of as what Jean-Claude Milner defines as 'thought' discussed above, because it involves producing something new and potentially making something visible that has been previously hidden. If the moment involves producing the subject in a new way then any idea of a natural subject is undermined and we instead see how enjoyment can form identity and make it appear natural. It is this enjoyment that shows us how we are constructed and it is this enjoyment that the Enjoyment Studies Degree to come would seek to explore.

4. Conclusion: 'To Enjoy or Not to Enjoy' and Illegal Enjoyment

'You read it? I suppose it changed your life, did it?' 'I suppose everything does. Even the morning paper, even the quiz on the back of the Special K box.'
– Lawrence Block[69]

This book began with the claim that we are now in a kind of second wave of what 19th-century Victorian discourse called 'rational recreation,' a project that attempted to both impose and regulate enjoyment in order to contain and limit revolutionary potential in its dissatisfied and potentially subversive subjects. A bizarre contributor to this discussion from that time, and someone who can still help the discussion today, is late 18th- and early 19th-century writer Jeremy Bentham. Bentham's theories of social control and organization have earned him a reputation as a repressive and reactionary man by followers of Michel Foucault, whose work involves an in-depth critique of Bentham's projects.[70] Nevertheless, Bentham's own work is subtle and important, particularly when it comes to happiness and enjoyment. For Bentham, every law should be productive of happiness. It's easy to see how this might link a couple of centuries forwards to Žižek and his idea of the law as productive of transgressive enjoyment, but of course Bentham's argument was not on the side of transgressive pleasure. For Bentham the law should be prohibitive in order to produce 'the greatest good for the greatest number,' in accordance with his philosophy of utilitarianism. Bentham argued for what he called the '*greatest happiness* principle' and writes that:

By utility is meant that property in any object, whereby it tends to produce benefit, advantage, pleasure, good, or happiness, (all this in the present case comes to the same thing) or (what comes again to the same thing) to prevent the happening of mischief, pain, evil, or unhappiness to the party whose interest is considered: if that party be the community in general, then the happiness of the community: if a particular individual, then the happiness of that individual.

Bentham created the 'felicific calculus,' an algorithm for calculating the amount of pleasure that a specific action is likely to cause and for comparing pleasure with pain to determine whether an act was in the service of moral good or evil.[71] In short, the theory holds that if the end result is more pleasurable than pain-inducing then the action is to be seen as in the service of moral good, whereas if more people feel pain than pleasure or if an individual feels more intense or durable pain than they do pleasure, then the act is in the service of evil. The association of pleasure with good connects to our present society characterized by a demand for constant enjoyment and suggests, like Schreber's comment that 'God demands a *constant state of enjoyment* [...] in keeping with the Order of Things,' that this apparently inherent link between pleasure and 'good' is a deeply rooted part of social organization. Many parts of our culture bear out the fact that this unconscious link between enjoyment and 'good' remains as central as ever, if not more so, from fridge magnets that remind us to enjoy ourselves when we are down, to pressuring friends to go on nights out against their will in the safe assumption that it will be 'good for them.' Bentham's work also inadvertently suggests that the category of 'happiness' is something on the side of the law, or something that can only exist under the imposition of law. The point here is that we have not come as far from Bentham as we like to think.

Sarah Ahmed's book *The Promise of Happiness* is a cultural critique of the imperative to be happy in our society, and it clearly links to the discussions of enjoyment here. Whilst happiness and enjoyment are two very different things, the similarities between them might be more important than the differences (Bentham sees them as one and the same in the quotation above). Discussing happiness in terms of gender politics, Ahmed has shown that 'the claim that women are happy, and that this happiness is behind the work they do, functions to justify gendered forms of labour not as products of nature, law or duty, but as an expression of a collective wish and desire.' For Ahmed, 'it is far from surprising that a recent study on happiness in the US suggested that feminist women are less happy than "traditional housewives"' because 'unhappiness' is a signifier of frustration and dissatisfaction with normalizing structures imposed and naturalized as if desired by all. She also argues that these structures of prescribed happiness very much serve the needs of capital.[72] We might think of the modern field of the 'science of happiness' and the numerous websites dedicated to promoting happiness in this light, as the ostensibly respectable wing of the regulation of enjoyment that has been discussed in this book. Categories of happiness discussed by such 'sciences' include institutions like marriage, presumed to have a positive impact on the happiness level of the subject, and other life choices justified to the subject on the grounds that they will 'make them happy.'

Happiness is measurable, like pleasure for Bentham, which could be measured by the seven categories of Intensity, Duration, Certainty, Propinquity, Fecundity, Purity and Extent. Unhappiness, on the other hand, is less measurable. This ideology goes as deep as the construction of language, where positive terms describe happiness and pleasure whilst the opposite can only be defined negatively by what it is not, as with the words *dis*pleasure, *un*happiness, *dis*satisfied and *un*enjoyable. Just as 'happiness' is a completely determined term, so too is 'enjoyment' a completely determined experience. A culture that thinks of itself as progressive has latched on to this research which aims to 'promote happiness' as a means of stipulating precisely what to enjoy, circumventing the problem that 'well, if it makes you happy, it must be good' seems to be a very thin basis for morality indeed. Happiness science seems to offer a way of telling people what should make them happy, ruling out those naughty things that should not. Likewise, enjoyment discourse tells us what we *ought* to enjoy and it also tells us what enjoyment we should see as acceptable, such as a game of Candy Crush, but also as 'useless' and ineffective, allowing it to operate on us in a different way whilst we think it is doing nothing but wasting our time. Further, enjoyment discourse works to justify actions on the grounds that we 'enjoy' them. It also, like the science of happiness, banishes some enjoyments entirely.

Some enjoyment is illegal. None of these enjoyments have been discussed in this book, and it would take quite a different book to do so. Yet, as a final suggestion, perhaps we might even say that something of Bentham's (albeit bizarre and problematic) collectivity has been lost, and that the enjoyment and happiness of society has been cut and marginalized in favor of the enjoyment of the individual. The fact that we place so much trust in our own individual enjoyment, seeing it as something positive and good, and something that is a 'gift of nature,' that is a reflection of 'who we are,' and that we can do nothing about, is very dangerous. This ideology of seeing enjoyment as a symptom of our 'nature' could lead to the following of passions found 'enjoyable' that are not only illegal but disastrous and damaging (it is probably best to avoid even giving an example here). A brilliant Louis Theroux documentary from 2007, *Behind Bars*, showed just how many inmates saw their 'natural enjoyment' of illegal things as the reason for their crimes.[73]

In my introduction I suggested that the existing discourses surrounding enjoyment may be politically dangerous in the sense that they help order and entrench a problematic class system, but it may also be that our discourses of enjoyment are *actually* dangerous too, promoting a feeling that desires should be followed and that enjoyment operates as its own justification for action because what we enjoy reflects who we naturally are. Instead I have tried to show here that enjoyment, and our attitudes towards it, creates who we are rather than reflecting our natural tendencies. In other words, I hope to have shown that a culture that tells us that our enjoyment is 'natural' can't very well complain when criminals turn up at the scene. Instead, if we come to see that our enjoyment is not 'what comes natural,' but something having an effect on us, constructing us as subjects, then we will not feel so obliged to follow what we enjoy and there will be no excuse for acting on forms of enjoyment that destroy the enjoyment and indeed safety of other people. I hope that my argument, albeit about Candy Crush and Football Manager, has this ethical dimension.

This book has suggested that there is an excess of enjoyment that is not determined and rationalized by our language and discourse despite its best attempts to rationalize and explain all of our pleasure. This enjoyment, which can be thought of in terms of what psychoanalysis calls *jouissance*, is not an outside to ideology or an enjoyment that escapes the rules of our ideology, but a moment which shows us something that our ideology would like to hide: that our enjoyment structures and constructs us as modern subjects rather than reflecting who we already are. Perhaps this is why Lacan can say that all *jouissance* is transgressive, because it not only involves crossing boundaries but creating new ones, changing us as subjects. This excessive enjoyment also therefore takes the subject into unknown futures which cannot always be explained by existing language, showing us that there is nothing 'natural' or secure about the identities produced, and that they can at least potentially be replaced by new identities. This unsecuring of the subject runs completely against the subjectivity that what I have thought of as a 'capitalist enjoyment discourse' would like to instill.

What could we do, faced with all this? Let's suppose that I am completely convinced by my own argument, that at least most enjoyment in our society has been rationalized and organized in such a way as to instill a sense of subjectivity that will suit a capitalist agenda? Would this make any of these enjoyments any less appealing? Would I stop enjoying Football Manager and start to enjoy only 'Gangnam Style'? It seems unlikely.

Yet, looking for moments of 'enjoyment' (often not particularly enjoyable or pleasurable ones) that we cannot explain as a reflection of already-existing ideas or conditions of subjectivity, can help explore the way in which we are constantly changing subjects, showing how enjoyment operates to construct us, and can therefore involve making our construction visible. We cannot decide when these moments are going to happen, so there is no way of calling one pleasure legitimate and productive and another illegitimate and unproductive, and no way of calling one enjoyment purely conformist and another completely radical. The most important point may be that no enjoyment is innocent and that it all operates on us in one way or another. As we find in the popular detective fiction of Lawrence Block, given as the epigraph to this conclusion, even the pleasure we get from the 'quiz on the back of the Special K box' operates on our subjectivity, and perhaps enjoyment is most dangerous at moments like this, when it appears not to be constructing us at all.

We can only enjoy what we enjoy, but look for the inconsistencies within it and be attentive to its power over us. It is with that excuse that we can close this book, open up Football Manager once more, and click that alluring and enticing button that leads off into an unknown future: 'Load Game'...

Endnotes

1. qtd. in Sigmund Freud, *The Standard Edition of the Complete Psychological Works of Sigmund Freud Vol 12*, trans. James Strachey (London: Vintage Books, 2001), p. 34.

2. For the major discussion of rational recreation see Peter Bailey, *Leisure and Class in Victorian England: Rational Recreation and the Contest for Control, 1830-1885* (New York: Routledge, 2007).

3. See, for example, Walter Benjamin, 'Theory of Distraction,' trans. Howard Eiland, in *The Work of Art in the Age of its Technological Reproducibility and Other Writings on Media*, pp. 56–7.

4. Ian Parker, Žižek: *An Introduction* (London: Pluto Press, 2004), p. 3.

5. For one of the most interesting discussions of the superego and modernity in Žižek's work see Slavoj Žižek, *The Parallax View* (Cambridge, MASS: MIT Press, 2006), pp. 187–90.

6. Jacques Lacan, *The Seminar of Jacques Lacan, Book X: Anxiety, 1962–1963*, unpublished manuscript, trans. Cormac Gallagher, session of 22 May 1963, p. 3.

7. Victoria Joy, '*Help!* I've got Comparison Anxiety,' in *Grazia Magazine*, 6/04/2015, pp. 55–7.

8. Todd McGowan, *The End of Dissatisfaction? Jacques Lacan and the Emerging Society of Enjoyment* (New York: SUNY Press, 2004), p. 3, 11.

9. Ibid., p. 34.

10. Mladen Dolar, 'Strel sredi koncerta,' in Theodor Adorno, *Uvod v sociologijo glasbe* (Ljubljana: DZS, 1986), p. 307.

11. Pierre Bourdieu, *Distinction: A Social Critique of the Judgement of Taste* (London: Routledge, 1986), p. 1, 3.

12. Walter Benjamin, *The Work of Art in the Age of its Technological Reproduction and Other Writings on Media* (London: Harvard

University Press, 2008), p. 57.

13. Matthew Arnold, *Culture and Anarchy* (Oxford: Oxford University Press, 2006), p. 5; F.R. Leavis, *Mass Civilization and Minority Culture* (Cambridge: Minority Press, 1930), pp. 3–4.

14. Terry Eagleton, *Literary Theory* (Oxford: Blackwell, 1996), pp. 9–10.

15. Michel Foucault, 'What is an Author?' in *Aesthetics, Method and Epistemology*, ed. James D. Faubion, trans. Robert Hurley (New York: The New Press, 1998), pp. 205–222 (p. 222).

16. For a fascinating discussion of the relationship between Deleuze and psychoanalysis see Gregg Lambert, 'De/Territorializing Psycho-analysis,' in Gabriele Schwab, ed., *Derrida, Deleuze, Psychoanalysis* (New York: Columbia University Press, 2007), pp. 192–212.

17. Giles Deleuze and Felix Guattari, *Anti-Oedipus,* trans. Robert Hurley, Mark Seem and Helen R. Lane (London: Continuum, 2000), p. 28.

18. Deleuze and Guattari, *Anti-Oedipus*, p. 28.

19. For a great discussion of these terms in relation to psycho-analysis see again Gregg Lambert, 'De/Territorializing Psychoanalysis,' in *Derrida, Deleuze, Psychoanalysis*, ed. Gabrielle Schwab (New York: Columbia University Press, 2008), pp. 192–212.

20. See also 'A Note on Feeling an Affinity with What You're Reading,' in EDA Collective, *Twerking to Turking* (Winchester and Washington: Zer0 Books, 2015), p. 42.

21. Deleuze and Guattari, *Anti-Oedipus*, pp. 29–30.

22. For an effective summary and a very useful book see Dylan Evans, *The Dictionary of Lacanian Psychoanalysis* (London: Routledge, 2006), p. 142.

23. Fredric Jameson, 'Foreword' to Jean-Francois Lyotard, *The Postmodern Condition*, trans. Geoff Bennington and Brian Massumi (Manchester: Manchester University Press, 2004),

pp. vii–xxii.

24. Jean-Francois Lyotard, *Libidinal Economy*, trans. Iain Hamilton Grant (London: Continuum, 1993), p. 5.
25. Ibid., p. 5.
26. Ibid., *Libidinal Economy*, p. 96.
27. Ibid., p. 94. For the major discussion of 'critique' see p. 6.
28. Jack Phillips in an interview about Football Manager carried out as research for this project.
29. On ADD and modern culture see Jonathan Crary, *Suspensions of Perception: Attention, Spectacle, and Modern Culture* (Cambridge, Mass: MIT Press, 2001), p. 35.
30. EDA Collective, 'How did the Other get so Big? The Swallowing of Democracy by the Imaginary Order: IDS, the big Public, and the Daily Mail,' in *Why Are Animals Funny?* (Winchester and Washington: Zer0 Books, 2014), pp. 111–3.
31. EDA Collective, 'Angry Birds and Postmodernism,' in *Why Are Animals Funny?*, pp. 65–6.
32. For the range of news outlets interested in this, regardless of their political alignment, see http://www.thesun.co.uk/sol/homepage/news/politics/4046753/David-Cameron-boasts-hes-finished-Angry-Birds-game.html ; and http://www.bbc.co.uk/schoolreport/17315004 ; and also http://www.theguardian.com/politics/shortcuts/2014/jan/24/david-camerons-top-downtime-tips
33. See Matthew d'Ancona, *In it Together: The Inside Story of the Coalition Government* (London: Penguin, 2013).
34. James Lyons, 'David Cameron's Angry Birds addiction may be a threat to the nation's security,' in *The Mirror*, 28/1/2014. Available at http://www.mirror.co.uk/news/uk-news/david-camerons-angry-birds-addiction-3086882.
35. For Baudrillard see for example Jean Baudrillard, *Simulacra and Simulacrum*, trans. Sheila Faria Glaser (Michigan: University of Michigan Press, 1994).
36. Here see the article published on Eurosport, https://uk.euros

port.yahoo.com/blogs/world-of-sport/student-lands-job-running-football-team-thanks-football-140446068.html

37. Iain Macintosh, Kenny Millar and Neil White, *Football Manager Stole My Life: 20 Years of Obsession* (Glasgow: BackPage Press, 2012).

38. Roland Barthes, *Mythologies*, trans. Annette Lavers (London: Vintage Classics, 2009).

39. Sigmund Freud, *The Complete Psychological Works of Sigmund Freud Volume 18*, trans. James Strachey (London: Hogarth Press, 1962), pp. 7–23 (p. 17).

40. Maurice Blanchot and Susan Hanson, *Yale French Studies*, no. 73 (1987), pp. 12–20 (p. 18).

41. For a study of the genealogy of cultural studies see Francis Mulhern, *Culture/Metaculture* (London: Routledge, 2000).

42. T. Brown, H. Rowley and K. Smith, 'Rethinking Research in Teacher Education,' in *British Journal of Educational Studies*, 62:3 (2014), pp. 281–96.

43. For a brilliant example of Adorno's work on popular culture see Theodor Adorno, 'Perrenial Fashion-Jazz,' in *Prisms*, (Cambridge, Mass: MIT Press, 1983), pp. 119–32.

44. See for example http://womens-studies.rutgers.edu/under-graduate/courses

45. http://www.theguardian.com/film/2015/apr/14/force-maje ure-films-philosophy-memento-ida-its-a-wonderful-life

46. Dylan Evans, *An Introductory Dictionary of Lacanian Psychoanalysis* (London: Routledge, 1996), pp. 91–2

47. Ibid., p. 92.

48. See EDA Collective, *Twerking to Turking: Everyday Analysis Volume Two* (Winchester and Washington: Zer0 Books, 2015), pp. 5–6.

49. Slavoj Žižek, *Event: Philosophy in Transit* (London: Penguin, 2014), p. 130-131.

50. Edward Said, *Orientalism* (London: Penguin, 1977).

51. Jens Erik Gould, 'Psy Talks 'Gangnam Style' and Newfound

Fame,' in *Time*, 28/9/2012), available at http://entertainment
.time.com/2012/09/28/psy-talks-gangnam-style-and-new-
found-fame/

52. Todd McGowan, *The End of Dissatisfaction?*, p. 4.

53. Maurice Blanchot and Susan Hanson, *Yale French Studies*, no.
73 (1987), pp. 12–20 (p. 18).

54. Chad William Timm, 'Stop the Madness!: Knowledge, Power
and Insanity in *A Song of Ice and Fire*,' in *Game of Thrones and
Philosophy*, pp. 264–77 (p. 266).

55. Greg Littmann, 'Maester Hobbes Goes to King's Landing,' in
Game of Thrones and Philosophy, ed. Henry Jacoby (Hoboken,
New Jersey: John Wiley and Sons, 2012), pp. 5–18 (p. 7).

56. Jean-Claude Milner, *L'Œuvre claire: Lacan, la science, la philo-
sophie* (Paris: Éditions du Seuil, 1995), p. 8 [my translation].

57. Jacques Lacan, 'The Tokyo discourse,' *Journal for Lacanian
Studies*, 3.1, (2005), pp. 129–44 (p. 32).

58. Slavoj Žižek, *Event*, p. 131.

59. Mark Fisher, *Capitalist Realism* (Winchester and Washington:
Zer0 Books, 2009), p. 60.

60. Robert Pfaller, *On the Pleasure Principle in Culture* (London:
Verso, 2014), p. 16–17.

61. Slavoj Žižek, *The Sublime Object of Ideology* (London: Verso,
1992), p. 35.

62. Pfaller, p. 17.

63. See Michel Foucault, *The History of Sexuality: The Will to
Knowledge Vol 1* (London: Penguin, 1998).

64. Roland Barthes, 'Striptease' in *Mythologies*, p. 97.

65. George R. R. Martin, *A Game of Thrones: A Song of Ice and Fire*
(London: Harper Collins, 2011), pp. 396-7.

66. Martin Jay, *Downcast Eyes: The Denigration of Vision in
Twentieth-Century French Thought* (London: University of
Nebraska Press, 1994), p. 51.

67. See Albert Cook, *Changing the Signs: The Fifteenth-Century
Breakthrough* (Lincoln, Nebraska: UNP, 1985).

68. Julia Kristeva, *Powers of Horror: An Essay on Abjection*, trans. Leon S. Roudiez (New York: Columbia University Press, 1984), pp. 1–11.

69. Lawrence Block, *The Burglar in the Rye* (Hapenden, Herts: No Exit Press, 1999), p. 175.

70. See Michel Foucault, *Discipline and Punish: The Birth of the Prison*, trans. Alan Sheridan (London: Penguin, 1977).

71. For Bentham's extensive discussion of pleasure and happiness see the first chapter of Jeremy Bentham, *An Introduction to the Principles of Morals and Legislation* (Oxford: Clarendon Press, 1907).

72. Sara Ahmed, 'Multiculturalism and the Promise of Happiness,' in *New Formations*, no. 63 (2007), pp. 121–37 (p. 121, 134). See also Sara Ahmed, *The Promise of Happiness* (Durham, NC: Duke University Press, 2010).

73. 'Louis Theroux: Behind Bars,' BBC (2007).

zero
books

Contemporary culture has eliminated both the concept of the public and the figure of the intellectual. Former public spaces – both physical and cultural – are now either derelict or colonized by advertising. A cretinous anti-intellectualism presides, cheerled by expensively educated hacks in the pay of multinational corporations who reassure their bored readers that there is no need to rouse themselves from their interpassive stupor. The informal censorship internalized and propagated by the cultural workers of late capitalism generates a banal conformity that the propaganda chiefs of Stalinism could only ever have dreamt of imposing. Zer0 Books knows that another kind of discourse – intellectual without being academic, popular without being populist – is not only possible: it is already flourishing, in the regions beyond the striplit malls of so-called mass media and the neurotically bureaucratic halls of the academy. Zer0 is committed to the idea of publishing as a making public of the intellectual. It is convinced that in the unthinking, blandly consensual culture in which we live, critical and engaged theoretical reflection is more important than ever before.

ZERO BOOKS

Capitalist Realism Is there no alternative?
Mark Fisher
An analysis of the ways in which capitalism has presented itself as the only realistic political-economic system.
Paperback: November 27, 2009 978-1-84694-317-1 $14.95 £7.99.
eBook: July 1, 2012 978-1-78099-734-6 $9.99 £6.99.

The Wandering Who? A study of Jewish identity politics
Gilad Atzmon
An explosive unique crucial book tackling the issues of Jewish Identity Politics and ideology and their global influence.
Paperback: September 30, 2011 978-1-84694-875-6 $14.95 £8.99.
eBook: September 30, 2011 978-1-84694-876-3 $9.99 £6.99.

Clampdown Pop-cultural wars on class and gender
Rhian E. Jones
Class and gender in Britpop and after, and why 'chav' is a feminist issue.
Paperback: March 29, 2013 978-1-78099-708-7 $14.95 £9.99.
eBook: March 29, 2013 978-1-78099-707-0 $7.99 £4.99.

The Quadruple Object
Graham Harman
Uses a pack of playing cards to present Harman's metaphysical system of fourfold objects, including human access, Heidegger's indirect causation, panpsychism and ontography.
Paperback: July 29, 2011 978-1-84694-700-1 $16.95 £9.99.

Weird Realism Lovecraft and Philosophy
Graham Harman
As Hölderlin was to Martin Heidegger and Mallarmé to Jacques
Derrida, so is H.P. Lovecraft to the Speculative Realist philoso-
phers.
Paperback: September 28, 2012 978-1-78099-252-5 $24.95 £14.99.
eBook: September 28, 2012 978-1-78099-907-4 $9.99 £6.99.

Sweetening the Pill or How We Got Hooked on Hormonal Birth
Control
Holly Grigg-Spall
Is it really true? Has contraception liberated or oppressed women?
Paperback: September 27, 2013 978-1-78099-607-3 $22.95 £12.99.
eBook: September 27, 2013 978-1-78099-608-0 $9.99 £6.99.

Why Are We The Good Guys? Reclaiming Your Mind From The
Delusions Of Propaganda
David Cromwell
A provocative challenge to the standard ideology that Western
power is a benevolent force in the world.
Paperback: September 28, 2012 978-1-78099-365-2 $26.95 £15.99.
eBook: September 28, 2012 978-1-78099-366-9 $9.99 £6.99.

The Truth about Art Reclaiming quality
Patrick Doorly
The book traces the multiple meanings of art to their various
sources, and equips the reader to choose between them.
Paperback: August 30, 2013 978-1-78099-841-1 $32.95 £19.99.

Bells and Whistles More Speculative Realism
Graham Harman
In this diverse collection of sixteen essays, lectures, and interviews
Graham Harman lucidly explains the principles of Speculative
Realism, including his own object-oriented philosophy.

Paperback: November 29, 2013 978-1-78279-038-9 $26.95 £15.99.
eBook: November 29, 2013 978-1-78279-037-2 $9.99 £6.99.

Towards Speculative Realism: Essays and Lectures Essays and Lectures
Graham Harman
These writings chart Harman's rise from Chicago sportswriter to co founder of one of Europe's most promising philosophical movements: Speculative Realism.
Paperback: November 26, 2010 978-1-84694-394-2 $16.95 £9.99.
eBook: January 1, 1970 978-1-84694-603-5 $9.99 £6.99.

Meat Market Female flesh under capitalism
Laurie Penny
A feminist dissection of women's bodies as the fleshy fulcrum of capitalist cannibalism, whereby women are both consumers and consumed.
Paperback: April 29, 2011 978-1-84694-521-2 $12.95 £6.99.
eBook: May 21, 2012 978-1-84694-782-7 $9.99 £6.99.

Translating Anarchy The Anarchism of Occupy Wall Street
Mark Bray
An insider's account of the anarchists who ignited Occupy Wall Street.
Paperback: September 27, 2013 978-1-78279-126-3 $26.95 £15.99.
eBook: September 27, 2013 978-1-78279-125-6 $6.99 £4.99.

One Dimensional Woman
Nina Power
Exposes the dark heart of contemporary cultural life by examining pornography, consumer capitalism and the ideology of women's work.
Paperback: November 27, 2009 978-1-84694-241-9 $14.95 £7.99.
eBook: July 1, 2012 978-1-78099-737-7 $9.99 £6.99.

Dead Man Working

Carl Cederstrom, Peter Fleming

An analysis of the dead man working and the way in which capital is now colonizing life itself.

Paperback: May 25, 2012 978-1-78099-156-6 $14.95 £9.99.

eBook: June 27, 2012 978-1-78099-157-3 $9.99 £6.99.

Unpatriotic History of the Second World War

James Heartfield

The Second World War was not the Good War of legend. James Heartfield explains that both Allies and Axis powers fought for the same goals - territory, markets and natural resources.

Paperback: September 28, 2012 978-1-78099-378-2 $42.95 £23.99.

eBook: September 28, 2012 978-1-78099-379-9 $9.99 £6.99.

Find more titles at www.zero-books.net